Seasons
of the Heart
and Home

Quilts *for a*
Winter's
Day
Jan Patek

American Quilter's Society

P. O. Box 3290 • Paducah, KY 42002-3290

ACKNOWLEDGMENTS

Special thanks to Kathy Glasco for calculating yardage and
to Nancy Crow for the use of some of her beautiful hand-dyed fabric.

All Quilt Photos: Richard Walker, Schenevus, NY.

All Quilts: Designed and constructed by Jan Patek;
quilted by Verna Graber and Jan Patek, under artist's supervision.

Library of Congress Cataloging-in-Publication Data

Patek, Jan.
    Quilts for a winter's day / Jan Patek.
        p.   cm. – (Seasons of the heart and home ; 2)
    ISBN 0-89145-824-7 : $18.95
    1. Quilting–Patterns.   2. Patchwork–Patterns.   3. Appliqué–
Patterns.   4. Patek, Jan–Diaries.   I. Title.   II Series.
TT835.P3855   1993
746.9'7–dc20   93–33043
                                                          CIP

Additional copies of this book may be ordered from:

American Quilter's Society
P.O. Box 3290
Paducah, KY 42002-3290
@18.95. Add $1.00 for postage and handling.

TABLE OF CONTENTS

INTRODUCTION

The last four years have been difficult for me. Like so many other women my age, I have been dealing with what are known as Empty Nest Syndrome, Mid-life Crisis, and Menopause.

My first book in the Seasons of the Heart and Home series, *Quilts for Summer Days,* dealt mainly with the "letting go" process that comes when the children grow up. For a lot of women twenty years or more of their life have revolved around raising children. Now that job is over and painful though the "letting go" process is, healing takes place and a new question forms: "Who am I?" Along with this there is the confusion and turmoil women go through emotionally and physically due to Menopause.

Quilts for a Winter's Day deals with my struggle to find my place in the world again. It is very important to me to feel that what I do day by day serves some purpose, has some meaning, helps in some way to make this a better world. This may be my heritage from Mennonite grandparents, it may be the way all of us feel, or it just may be me – I don't know. I suspect somehow that all of us need this.

Part of my adapting and coping has been to bring my quilting with me through the changes – and in fact use it as a vehicle to understand myself and the changes.

Out of these fall and winter days has come this book. *Quilts for a Winter's Day* is about resting, and taking time to focus on myself and what is important to me. It's about resting and rocking and gathering strength.

THE JOURNAL / THE QUILTS

The need to get out is lessening
and the need to burrow in
is coming on strong....

"The Bray House," 55½" x 56½". See page 38 for pattern.

24 October 92

I love this time of year.

We're having a real Indian Summer. Max and Brian are home for the weekend. I've got spaghetti started for dinner tonight and Kelly's coming in to pick up pumpkins and have dinner.

Hazel and I went to Jamesport yesterday and got pumpkins – nine in all – for kids, boyfriends, girlfriends and roommates. Max said he'd carve his pumpkin and leave it here instead of taking it to the dorm. That's good. I forgot to get one for us and the ones we grew have already been given away or are being used as decorations.

The cornfields are beautiful – either a golden tan, moving and rustling in the wind – or harvested and silent – golden brown and dark brown, resting until spring.

The trees are a blaze of color.

No grass to mow, no hay to throw yet. All I have to do is feed the animals and quilt.

I love this time of year!

"Caldwell County," 52½" x 69½". See page 42 for pattern.

9 November 92

I always seem to have this interesting juxtaposition between the traditional and the innovative. I've been trying to draw a new block for my Christmas tablecloth and I have finally given up. I like the block I have drawn but what I see inside my head – what I want – is traditional. I want Coxcombs and Currants and a Partridge in a Pear Tree – done differently.

I think the need for tradition speaks to something. Things are changing so fast these days – nothing seems stable. I think that "home" is one of the values that we need to hold onto. When the kids were here we always tried to have dinner together "without television." So I shall make a traditional cloth for the table in somewhat non-traditional material.

And I guess I'm making a pheasant in a currant bush instead of a partridge in a pear tree. Partridges are small gray birds, Pep tells me, and in my eyes that doesn't go with Christmas. Even the currants are really grape size. Ah well, you need to give tradition a twist to make it your own.

"Holiday Tablecloth," 62½" x 62½". See page 52 for pattern.

11 November 92

"I have written every poem, every novel, for the same purpose –
to find out what I think, to know where I stand."
(May Sarton, _Journal of a Solitude_*)

And I might add – to know who I am.

I have been feeling sad the last few days and don't know why.
It's as if there were something missing, some sense of purpose. My
purpose was raising kids, providing them with a home so that they
would have what they needed. So – who am I now? What do I do?
What is my function? Why am I important?

17 November 92

Today we'll put some more poultry in the freezer. That always gives
me such a secure feeling. There's food for the winter and everything
is taken care of. The need to get out is lessening and the need to
burrow in is coming on strong.

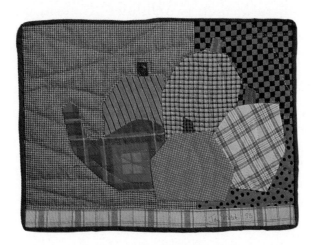

"Fall Placemats," 17" x 12". See page 62 for patterns.

26 November 92

"How can I be sure that all the years I have sat at a desk add up to anything worth having as against what I might have done had I, for instance, devoted myself to teaching underprivileged children?" (May Sarton, <u>Plant Dreaming Deep</u>*)

Self-doubt or self-indulgence? I don't know. I feel floaty and disjointed. The pressure of time is still here. I thought that when the children were gone the pressure would mainly be gone. But now I'm middle aged and as May Sarton says, "time seemed to shrink." So little time left to achieve anything.

30 November 92

It's snowing and I need to get to work. I'm patching an old quilt that I love and putting it on the bed in Brian's room. He used it constantly and it's tattered in places. But I love it; it's one of my favorite quilts. I think quilts look neat somewhat tattered but Kelly is bringing a friend home for Thanksgiving (named Brian also), and I don't want him to think I have given him a torn up quilt.

I keep patting the quilt as I work. Like me, it's somewhat worn but still useful. It says things about the place of hard work and beauty in this world and keeps people warm too.

"Autumn Leaves," 21" x 24½". See page 64 for pattern.

18 December 92

I don't feel as if it's Christmas, and then again, I do. I hope they come today and put up the mantel I found. Then I can decorate it and feel the decorating's done.

Almost all of the stuff that can be a hassle is taken care of. I think I've found things that everyone will like. Scheduling is turning out to be the biggest problem. Christmas can get exhaustingly complex with families so scattered – Kelly & Max in St. Joe, Church in Kansas City and a 6:00 a.m. Julotta service. Brian has to go to Liberal and will only make it in late Christmas for dinner. And there's Pep's father in Chillicothe and my mother in Kansas City. No wonder I'm feeling so stretched. There are so many people we want to be with, to share the time of year.

I think that that's part of what my quilt "Silent Night" means. That love is the hub – the vine that weaves it all together. That love is what it's all about. I needed to stop, write this down and stare at my quilt to get back in touch with why we're doing all of this. It's time to get it on the wall so I can see that every day.

"Silent Night," 53" x 69". See page 66 for pattern.

4 January 93

Matthew's reindeer is really neat. I like the wallhanging and placemats. I bought the material in the center of the placemat with a star years ago because it reminded me of Grandma Laird's wallpaper. And I bought it in a little store in Salem, Indiana, where my Grandma Berkey lived. Both Grandmas and a nephew in one placemat!

"Santa Table Runner," 44" x 30". See page 80 for pattern.

5 January 93

Why do I love being alone so much? I almost feel guilty about it.

"Santa Placemats," 17" x 15". See pages 84-85 for patterns.

7 January 93

The first snowfall of the winter. Bill Turner came yesterday and brought a large bale of hay for Suzie and Benny. They're happily munching away and walk to their pole barn when the north wind hits too hard.

The swans are chafing at being in the poultry yard but they're safe from coyotes until the pond thaws. They look wistfully at the gate and make irritated noises at me.

The chickens, ducks and geese go on with life as usual – snow means little to them. Softly falling snow and chickens clucking are two of the most peaceful sounds in the world. I went to the chicken yard for a while this afternoon just to listen. Jeanne Nelson says that chickens sing. I think she's right.

"Santa Wallhanging," 26" x 36". See page 88 for pattern.

10 January 93

We're snowed in! I love it. Brian got over yesterday and helped me get two bales of straw into the shed for Suzie and Benny. Then he barely got out before the drifts cut us off. Pep said it finally stopped snowing around midnight. Sitting in my chair quilting, I can see the huge cedars laden with snow at the top of the hill. I wonder how old they are? They were that big when we built the house 22 years ago. The first contractor said he'd have to take out all of the big trees. We found another contractor.

So my cedars are still here to greet me every morning as the sun rises. I wonder what trees mean to us? They've figured prominently in women's quilts for years.

Maybe they're a symbol of continuity and life. Like our quilts, they're beautiful as well as useful and they go on long after we do. Who planted them — or just didn't mow them? Was it the Arnetts or Dices who lived here before we did? I know that the Pateks transplanted Missouri Red Cedars all along the road. It really doesn't matter who planted them. They're here.

My, I'm getting fanciful. Snow does that to me. I'm going to feed the animals, then stomp my way back in and quilt, quilt, quilt till Brian shovels us out or the road maintainer comes.

"Snowflakes & Cedars," 59" x 84". See page 90 for pattern.

13 January 93

Snow and ice. And cold. We got some chains for the first time in years because of all of the ice. It's going to be that kind of winter.

Right now I'm finding it difficult to quilt or write because I keep staring out the window. The sun is out for the first time in days — it's clean and cold — and all of the branches are covered with ice on top of the snow. When I did the chores icicles rained on me every time the wind blew. The ground glitters with the fallen slivers.

Mr. Cat (Miss Katrina turned out to be a boy) is purring, keeping my lap warm as I try to quilt and drink coffee. But I keep stopping and staring out of the window. Snow, ice, trees, and sky. I've never particularly wanted to do a two-tone quilt — or quilts with much white in them for that matter. But I want to try to catch the feeling of this.

Different shades of dark — dark green, brown green, black brown, black blue, blue. And whites and soft grays, with gray blues. White plaids and prints for shadows. "Winter Solstice," a time of peace and beauty.

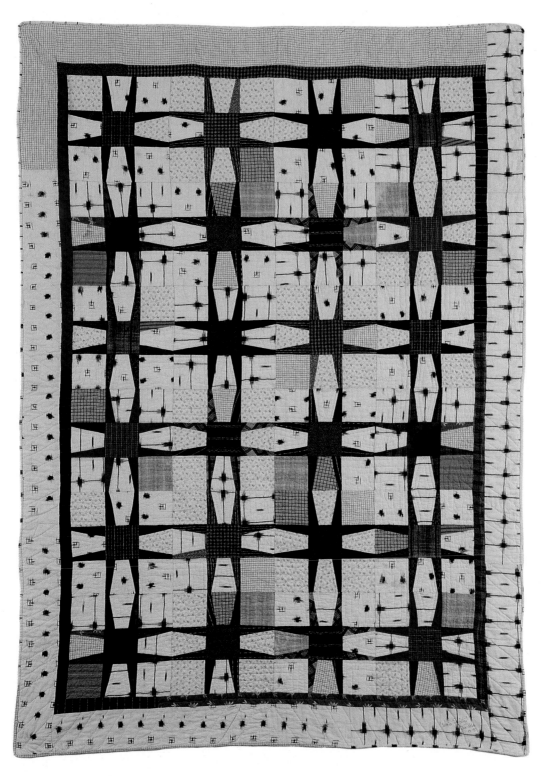

"Winter Solstice," 60" x 84". See page 100 for pattern.

25 January 93

I got the background blocked in for "Seraphim" during the Inauguration but it was noon Saturday before I had the angels, wings and trumpets in place. Two mornings with no appliqué or quilting! I felt lost! It's amazing how much quilting is an integrating factor in my life. I've adjusted a lot to the changes and cataclysms that come with Mid-life, Empty Nest Syndrome, and Menopause, but there are still quite a few tremors. Appliquéing in the morning is a portion of my life that is stable. Part of my adapting and coping has been to bring my quilting with me through the changes – and in fact use it as a vehicle to understand myself and the changes. I don't like being without it.

I've always put a guardian angel in family quilts. I like the angels in this quilt. They are primitive and somehow look powerful to me. I need a whole flock of guardian angels to watch over the dispersed family, and I don't want wimpy little things either.

"Seraphim," 43" x 55". See page 103 for pattern.

30 January 93

Dr. Van Buskirk — such a remarkable man — retired yesterday. Not only did I work for him when I got married and had my children but he is the only doctor that I have ever really gone to.

I have no idea what to do or where to go, right when all of this estrogen, Menopause dilemma is upon me. He listened, really listened to his patients. His sense of compassion and his expertise are going to be very hard to replace. I will miss him — as a doctor and as a friend.

1 February 93

I'm still uncertain as to what function my art and quilts serve in this world. It does make me angry that Menopause and Mid-Life Crisis have been pretty well ignored until recently and that the Empty Nest Syndrome is made light of. Basically, most women's lives are made light of. I guess that's what I want to record. I want somehow to say — "Hey! This is what life is made of for most of us. It's important! Home and children, coping when they leave, Menopause, the struggle to feel worthwhile and good about ourselves when we don't look like Cher and don't have 'exciting' lives."

"Seraph," 21" x 14". See page 105 for pattern.

17 February 93

Two really stressing days! I need a day off. Letting go is so difficult! Unsettled – ragged edges – things jumbled and not in place – stressed.

There is so much going on that is just out of my control. The kids are dealing with things that they have to overcome on their own. It's not like when they were little and I could tuck them in bed and then check on them.

So today I shall cut my little snowpersons out, and make them their own little world where I still have some control. But heck – the snowpersons will probably grow up and decide to be dentists, psychologists and engineers, or God knows what, and off they will go, too.

Well, I will have to create something new then.

"Snowman Placemat," 18" x 13". See page 108 for patterns.

"Snowman Wallhanging," 19" x 27". See page 110 for pattern.

"Snowman Stocking," 17¼" x 22". See page 112 for patterns.

15 March 93

Worked on "The Sperry Quilt" all day and it's finished except for the border. When I work on a quilt as complex as this, at the end I always feel as if there were a steel rod next to my backbone, holding me up straight while I pull everything together. All the muscles in my back are relaxing now, one by one.

When I finished, I walked down to the pond dam to give the swans some corn and kick a hole in the ice for them. (Earendil is sitting on a nest in the snow, silly thing.)

As I walked down the hill I was struck again by the richness and diversity of color in the winter. Fall and winter are by far my favorite times of the year. The colors are all there, they just don't scream at you. Touches in birds, bits of grass, berries, trees, winter wheat — that's what "The Sperry Quilt" is all about.

"The Sperry Quilt," 54" x 54". See page 118 for pattern.

"Winter Solstice (small)," 14" x 18". See page 140 for pattern.

3 April 93

"Experiencing menopause as a 'soul event' as well as a body event opens us to a more inclusive way of journeying through this passage. For there is surely grief and darkness in the letting go of our fruit-bearing years. But there is also a release in letting go of the old which makes way for the new – truly the journey of change; that too involves risk and venturing into the unknown."
(Joan Borton, Women of the 14th Moon Writings on Menopause*)

Virago – original meaning – strong, experienced, and wise older woman. Crone and hag – I am liking the sounds of even those words. What is wrong with getting older? Or even old? We all have to do it.

"While we cannot change our society's attitudes towards us, we can change our attitude toward ourselves."
(Maureen Williams, Women of the 14th Moon Writings on Menopause**)

*Joan Borton, Women of the 14th Moon: Writings on Menopause, edited by Dena Taylor and Amber Coverdale Sumrall, The Crossing Press, 1991, p. 363. Used by permission of The Crossing Press.

**Maureen Williams, Women of the 14th Moon: Writings on Menopause, edited by Dena Taylor and Amber Coverdale Sumrall, The Crossing Press, 1991, p. 361. Used by permission of The Crossing Press.

9 April 93

What am I doing anything for?

Why does there have to be a "for?"

Why make art?

Why are we here? Why are we alive?

I don't know. Before, I was raising children.

10 April 93

"Completing long endeavors, such as finishing school, concluding a manuscript, fulfilling one's opus, caregiving an ill person, all these have their times when the once-young energy turns old, falls down and can go on no longer.

For women it is best if they understand this at the outset of an endeavor, for women tend to be surprised by fatigue. Then they wail, they mutter, they whisper about failure, inadequacy and such. No. No. This losing of energy is as it is. It is Nature . . ."

"But in the end, a woman must rest now, rock now, regain her focus."

Both from Women Who Run With the Wolves*

*Clarissa Pinkola Estés, PhD., Women Who Run With the Wolves, Ballentine Books, 1992, p. 331. Used by permission of Ballentine Books.

I can see a woman in a rocking chair inside the house in "Snowflakes and Cedars" and "Silent Night," rocking and resting and gathering strength. She probably has her quilting hoop by her side or a bag of appliqué or piecing to do. The touch — the tactile part is soothing. She rocks and she rests and she quilts. I think that's what my winter quilts are all about — resting and pondering and gathering strength....

PROJECTS & PATTERNS SECTION

Complete patterns and instructions for making the quilts, wallhangings, tablecloths, and placemats pictured with journal entries are included in this section, occasionally with slight changes in overall measurements for easy use of instructions. Keep the following in mind as you work with the patterns and instructions:

(+sa) = plus seam allowance. All patterns pieces and measurements need to have ¼" seam allowance added. The lines given in the patterns are sewing lines, not cutting lines.

Borders – As each of us sews a little differently, I would suggest measuring your quilt before cutting the borders for which I have given you measurements. Most of the time, I am sure that we will agree but occasionally....

Patterns – Keep in mind that these are folk-style patterns, which have a very personal style to them. I encourage you to use the patterns and my quilts' layouts as a starting place. Relax, experiment, and have fun creating your own version of each quilt. Add a second cat to the design if you have two! Include your son as well!

As this is a pattern book and, therefore, general instructions for appliqué, piecing, and quilting techniques are not included, you may want to consult your favorite publications for assistance in these areas. The following books available from AQS (toll-free 1-800-626-5420) would also be helpful:

For general techniques:
From Basics to Binding by Karen Kay Buckley
Quiltmaker's Guide by Carol Doak
Classic Basket Quilts by Marianne Fons & Elizabeth Porter

For appliqué:
Appliqué Designs: My Mother Taught Me to Sew by Faye Anderson
The Art of Appliqué by Laura Lee Fritz

For quilting:
The Ins and Outs: Perfecting the Quilting Stitch by Patricia Morris
Quilting with Style by Gwen Marston & Joe Cunningham

The house in this quilt and some of the other quilts in this book are based loosely on the "Bray" house. Stan and Charlotte Bray, like us, live out in the country and last year they built a new house on the site of their old one. All summer, those of us who take Highway BB into town and back got to watch the progress of their house. It turned out to be a jewel of a house, soft gray with white trim, a white porch, and a beautiful wood door.

I think it so struck me for a number of reasons. First, it is beautiful. Secondly, in the midst of rolling hills, it sits on top of one of the few open places and it feels like you can see for miles around it. Thirdly, it seems to be just the right size for the two of them. Not too large, not too small — just right — cozy and inviting and speaking of home.

For this last reason it has become the part of a lot of the quilts in this book.

THE BRAY HOUSE
55½" x 56½" finished size

FABRIC REQUIREMENTS

Houses
  ¼ yd for each house – 6 different prints

Roofs
  ¼ yd for each roof – 6 different prints

Backgrounds
  ¼ yd for each background – 6 different prints

Sashing
  1 yd for sashing (pieced)
  1⅓ yd for sashing (without piecing)

Borders
  ¼ yd for inner border
  1 yd for outer border

Binding
  ¼ yd for straight binding

INSTRUCTIONS (Pattern: page 142)
- Piece 3 house blocks and 3 reverse house blocks in the following sequence:
- a, b, c
- Sew above to d
- e, f
- g, h, i
- Sew above to d
- j, k, l
- Sew to house
- Cut 4 – 17" x 3½" sashing (+sa) strips
- Connect house blocks and reverse house blocks with sashing strips as follows:
    Reverse house – House
    17" x 3½" strip – 17" x 3½" strip
    Reverse house – House
    17" x 3½" strip – 17" x 3½" strip
    Reverse House – House
- Cut 3 – 38½" x 3½" (+sa) sashing strips
- Connect rows of house with 38½" x 3½" strip
- Sew remaining two 38½" x 3½" strips to sides
- Cut two 44½" x 3½" (+sa) sashing strips

- Sew 44½" x 3½" strips to top and bottom
- Cut 2 borders 44½" x 1" (+sa)
- Cut 2 borders 47½" x 1" (+sa)
- Sew 44½" x 1" borders to top and bottom
- Sew 47½" x 1" borders to sides
- Cut 2 borders 47½" x 4½" (+sa)
- Cut 2 borders 55½" x 4½" (+sa)
- Sew 47½" x 4½" borders to sides
- Sew 55½" x 4½" borders to top and bottom
- Quilt and bind.

Full Quilt Diagram

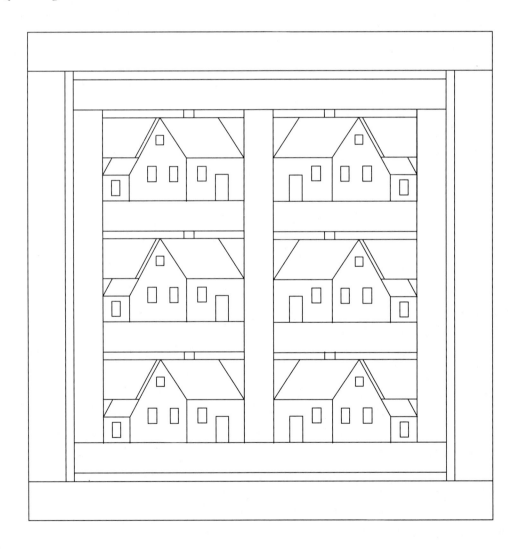

Placement Diagram

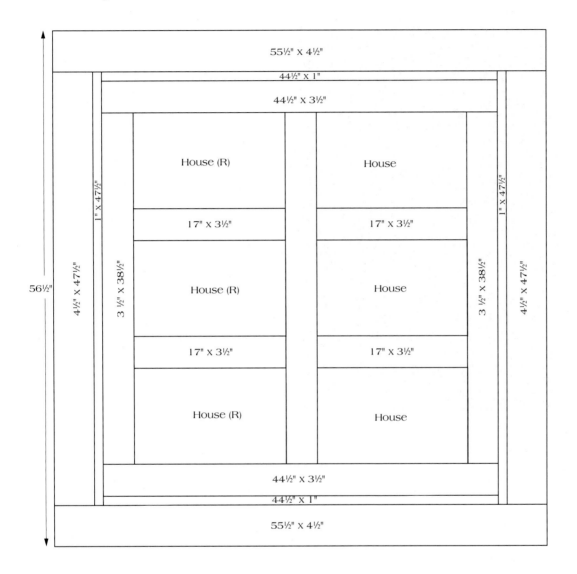

55½" x 4½"

44½" x 1"

44½" x 3½"

House (R)

House

17" x 3½"

17" x 3½"

House (R)

House

17" x 3½"

17" x 3½"

House (R)

House

44½" x 3½"

44½" x 1"

55½" x 4½"

56½"

4½" x 47½"

3 ½" x 38½"

1" x 47½"

1" x 47½"

3 ½" x 38½"

4½" x 47½"

Page 142

CALDWELL COUNTY
52½" x 69½" finished size

FABRIC REQUIREMENTS
1⅜ yd total of mediums & darks for background

¼ yd black for background sashing

⅛ yd of 7 different lights, mediums, and darks for top and bottom borders

1 yd of light for light sashing, inner and outer border

Scraps stripped for middle side borders

¼ yd or fat quarter for trees

¼ yd for each house

¼ yd for each roof

¼ yd or fat quarter for pumpkins and squash

Scraps for corn, leaves, cats, and flying geese

INSTRUCTIONS (Patterns: pages 44-45, 49-50, 142, 147-148, 151)
- Piece background according to **Diagram #1**.
- Cut 1 house block, omitting pieces j & l. Appliqué windows, door and chimney in place.
- Cut 1 reverse house, roof, chimney, windows, and door only. Omit background of house block.
- Cut 1 cat and 1 reverse cat.
- Cut 5 cornstalks. Line stalks 1, 2, & 3. (I turned the seam allowance under for both the stalk and the lining, put wrong sides together and used a buttonhole stitch to sew them together. Cut a total of 8 corn leaves, 3x, 1x(r), 2y and 2y(r). Cut a lining for 1y and 2y(r). Lining pattern is the same as leaf pattern only reversed. I lined these the same way I lined the cornstalks, turned under seam allowances, wrong sides together, buttonhole stitched together. Appliqué cornstalks and leaves behind house as seen in **Diagram #2**.
- Cut and piece flying geese as seen in **Diagram #4**.
- Cut 2 falling leaves and 1 reverse falling leaf.

- Cut trees and pumpkins.
- Appliqué all in place according to photo.
- Strip piece top and bottom borders, starting with 44½" x 2" (+sa) light sashing and then using various widths of 7 different lights and darks for a total border of 44½" x 8" (+sa). Sew one 8" border to top and one to the bottom of background piece with light sashing material towards background piece. (See **Diagram #3**) Cut 4 – 66½" x 1½" (+sa) light borders (same material as light sashing strips).
- Cut 2 – 66½" x 1" (+sa) borders of strip pieced material from background and top and bottom borders.
- Sew into two side borders – 66" x 1½" light sashing, 66" x 1" striped pieced, 66" x 1½" light sashing (See **Diagram #3**)
- Sew 3 piece borders to sides
- Cut 2 – 52½" x 2" (+sa) borders of light sashing material
- Sew 52½" x 2" borders to top and bottom
- Quilt and bind.

Diagram #1

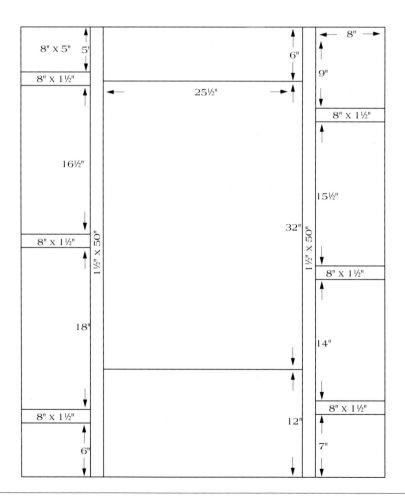

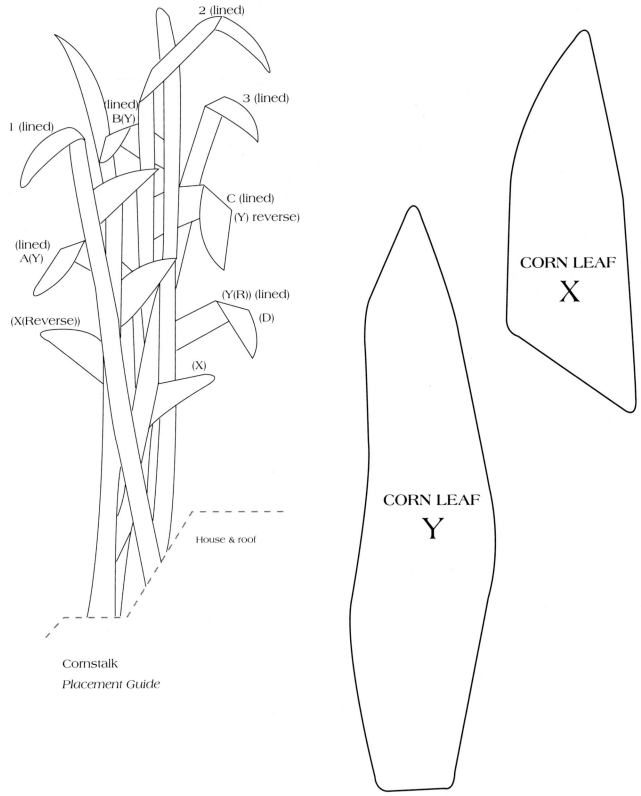

Diagram #2

2 (lined)

3 (lined)

(lined) B(Y)

1 (lined)

C (lined)
(Y) reverse

(lined) A(Y)

(Y(R)) (lined)
(D)

(X(Reverse))

(X)

House & roof

Cornstalk
Placement Guide

CORN LEAF
X

CORN LEAF
Y

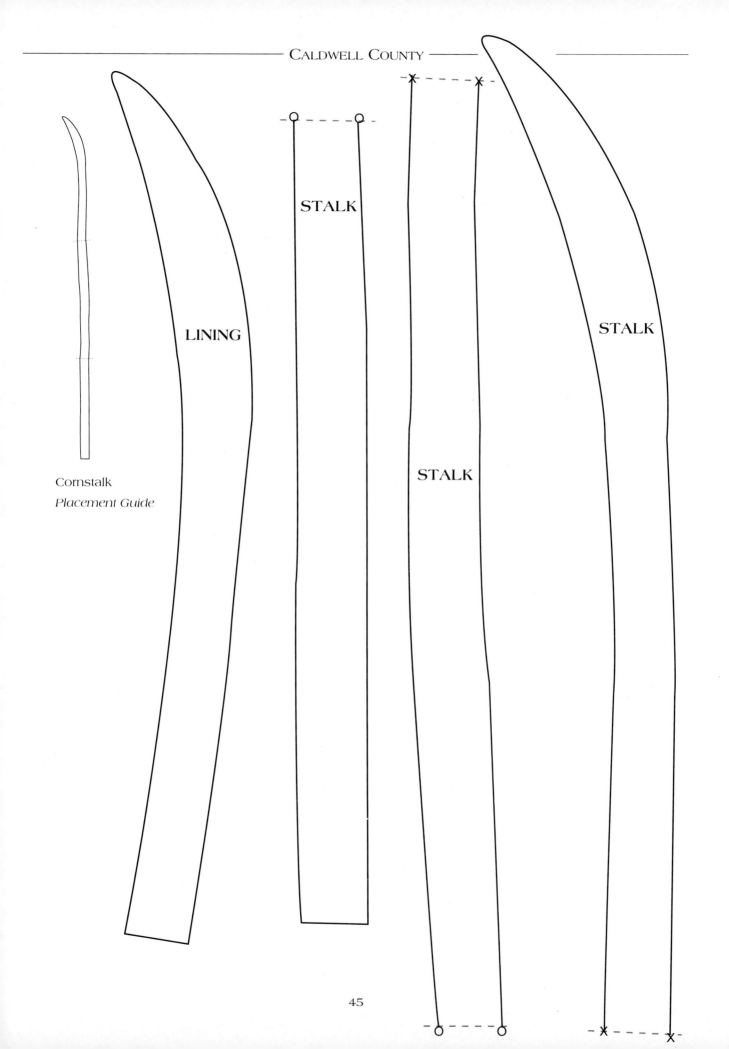

Cornstalk
Placement Guide

LINING

STALK

STALK

STALK

STALK

Diagram #3

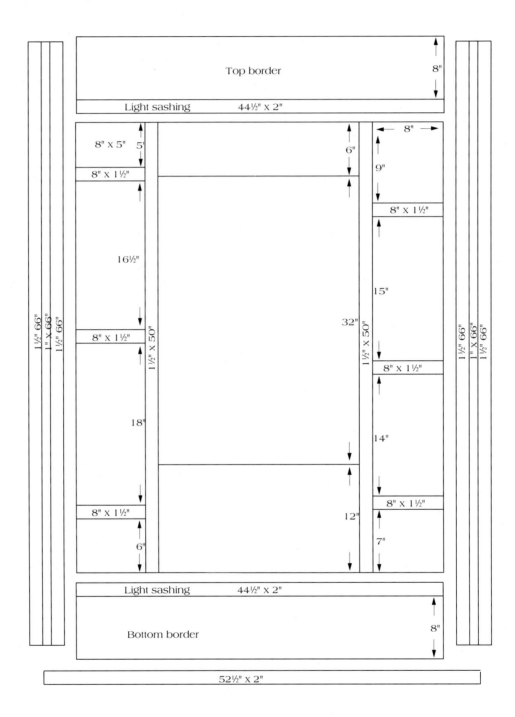

Background Diagram

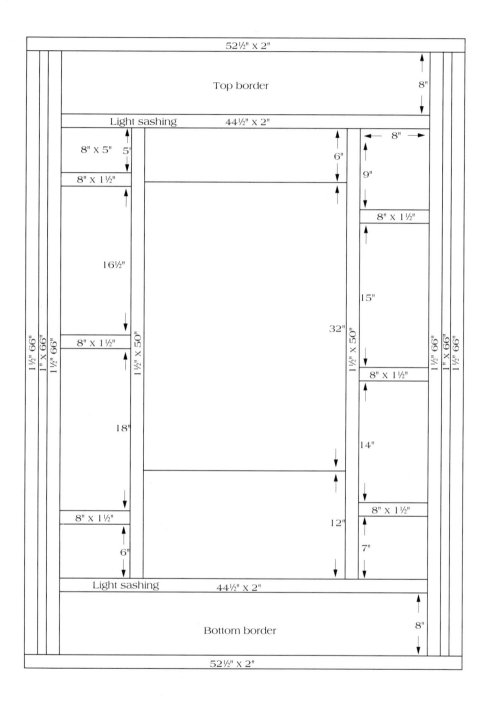

52½" x 2"

Top border

8"

Light sashing   44½" x 2"

8" x 5"   5"

6"

8" x 1½"

8"

9"

8" x 1½"

16½"

15"

32"

1½" x 50"

8" x 1½"

8" x 1½"

18"

14"

1½" 66"
1" x 66"
1½" 66"

1½" x 50"

1½" 66"
1" x 66"
1½" 66"

8" x 1½"

12"

8" x 1½"

6"

7"

Light sashing   44½" x 2"

Bottom border

8"

52½" x 2"

Page 142

Page 147

Page 148

Page 151

Diagram #4

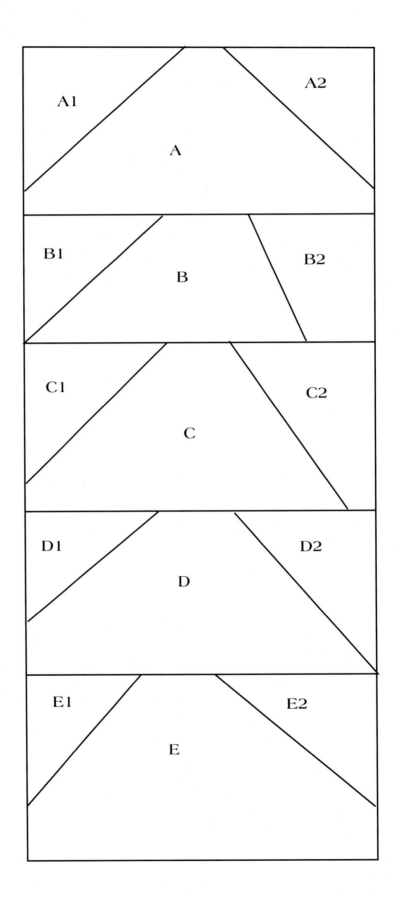

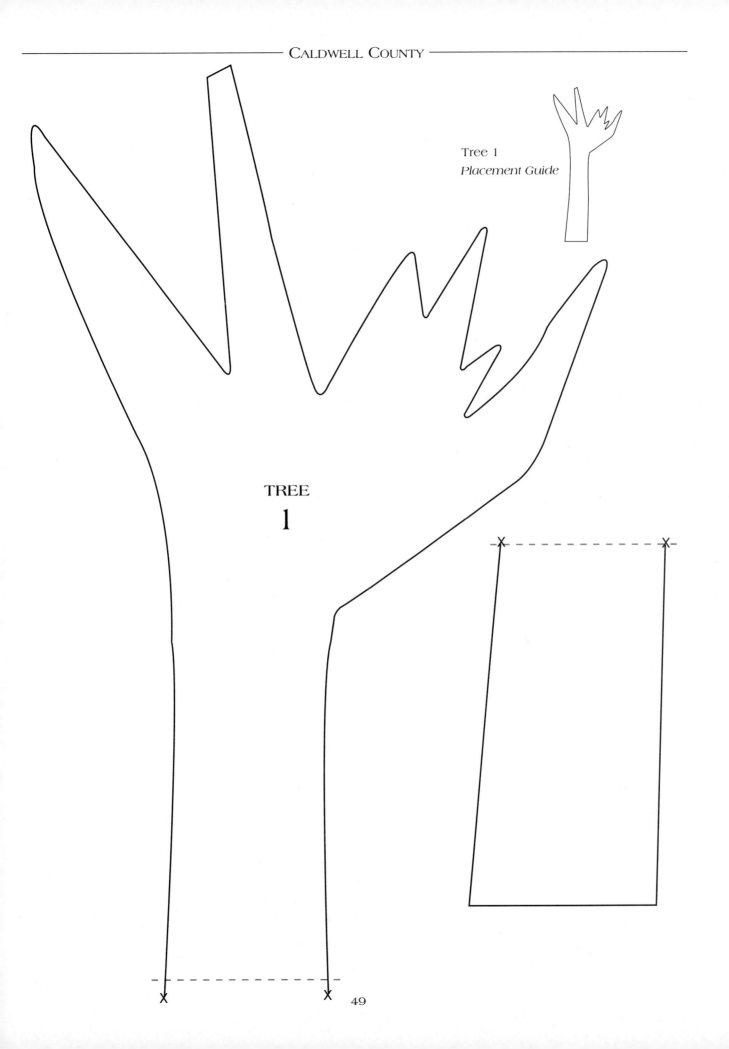

Tree 1
Placement Guide

TREE
1

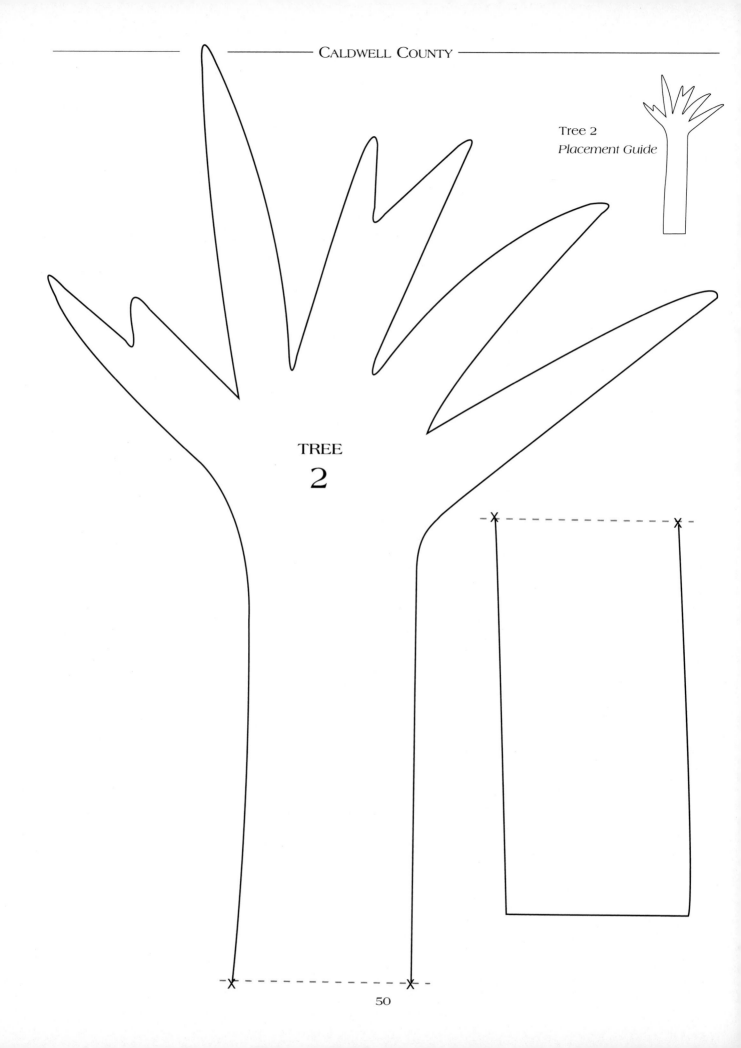

Tree 2
Placement Guide

TREE
2

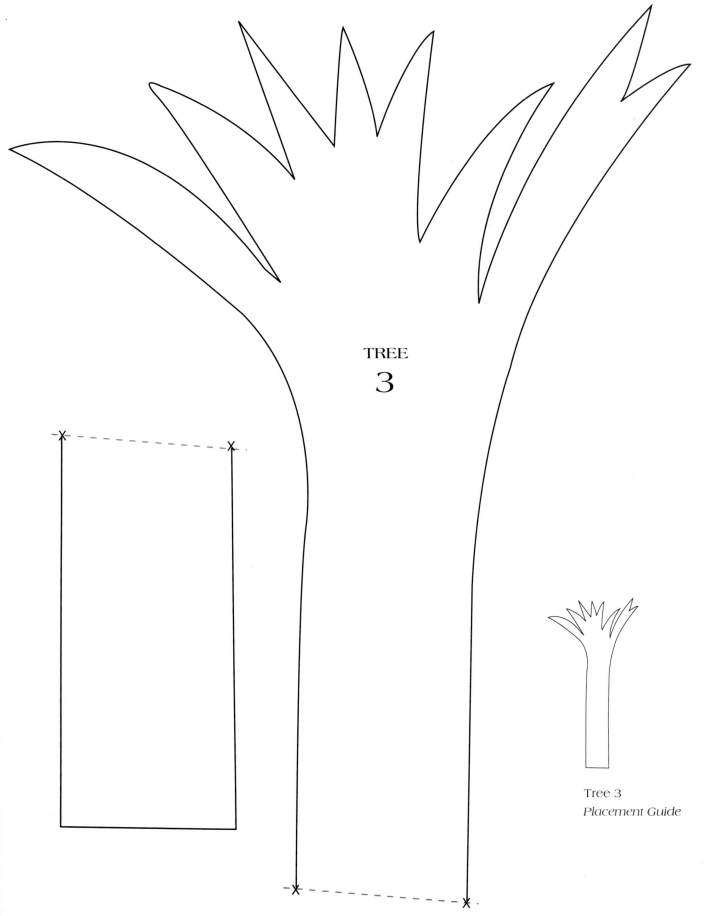

TREE
3

Tree 3
Placement Guide

HOLIDAY TABLECLOTH
62½" x 62½" finished size

FABRIC REQUIREMENTS
1¼ yd of background fabric
2 yds each of red, gold, and green
4 yds backing fabric

INSTRUCTIONS (Patterns: pages 54-55, 58-61, 70-71)
- Cut 4 – 20" (+sa) blocks
- Appliqué Coxcombs and Currants on 2 blocks
  Use 8 – 10" x ¼" (+sa) bias strips for vines
- Appliqué Pheasant in a Currant Bush on 2 blocks
- Cut 4 – 20" x 1½" (+sa) red border strips
- Cut 4 – 20" x 1½" (+sa) gold border strips
- Cut 2 – 20" x 1½" (+sa) green border strips
- Assemble 2 – 20" x 7½" borders with strips in the following order: (see **Diagram #1**)
  Red, Gold, Green, Gold, Red
- Join blocks in 2 vertical rows with a 20" x 7½" border between blocks. (See **Diagram #1**)
  Row 1: Pheasant Block, Border, Coxcombs and Currants Block
  Row 2: Coxcombs and Currants Block, Border, Pheasant Block
- Cut 6 – 47½" x 1½" (+sa) red border strips
- Cut 6 – 47½" x 1½" (+sa) gold border strips
- Cut 3 – 47½" x 1½" (+sa) green border strips
- Assemble 3 – 47½" x 7½" borders with strips in the following order: (see **Diagram #1**)
  Red, Gold, Green, Gold, Red
- Join vertical rows of blocks with a 47½" x 7½" border. (See **Diagram #1**)
- Sew remaining 2 – 47½" x 7½" borders to sides
- Cut 4 – 62½" x 1½" (+sa) red border strips
- Cut 4 – 62½" x 1½" (+sa) gold border strips
- Cut 2 – 62½" x 1½" (+sa) green border strips

• Assemble 2 – 62½" x 7½" borders with strips in the following order: (See **Diagram #1**)
Red, Gold, Green, Gold, Red
• Sew 62½" x 7½" border to top and bottom

As this was for use as a tablecloth, I didn't use batting between the pieced top and the backing. I was surprised at how nicely the quilting stitches looked even without batting. If you want to use this as a throw or wallhanging, I would suggest a low loft batt and you might want the currant bush to be square on the block instead of at an angle.

Diagram #1

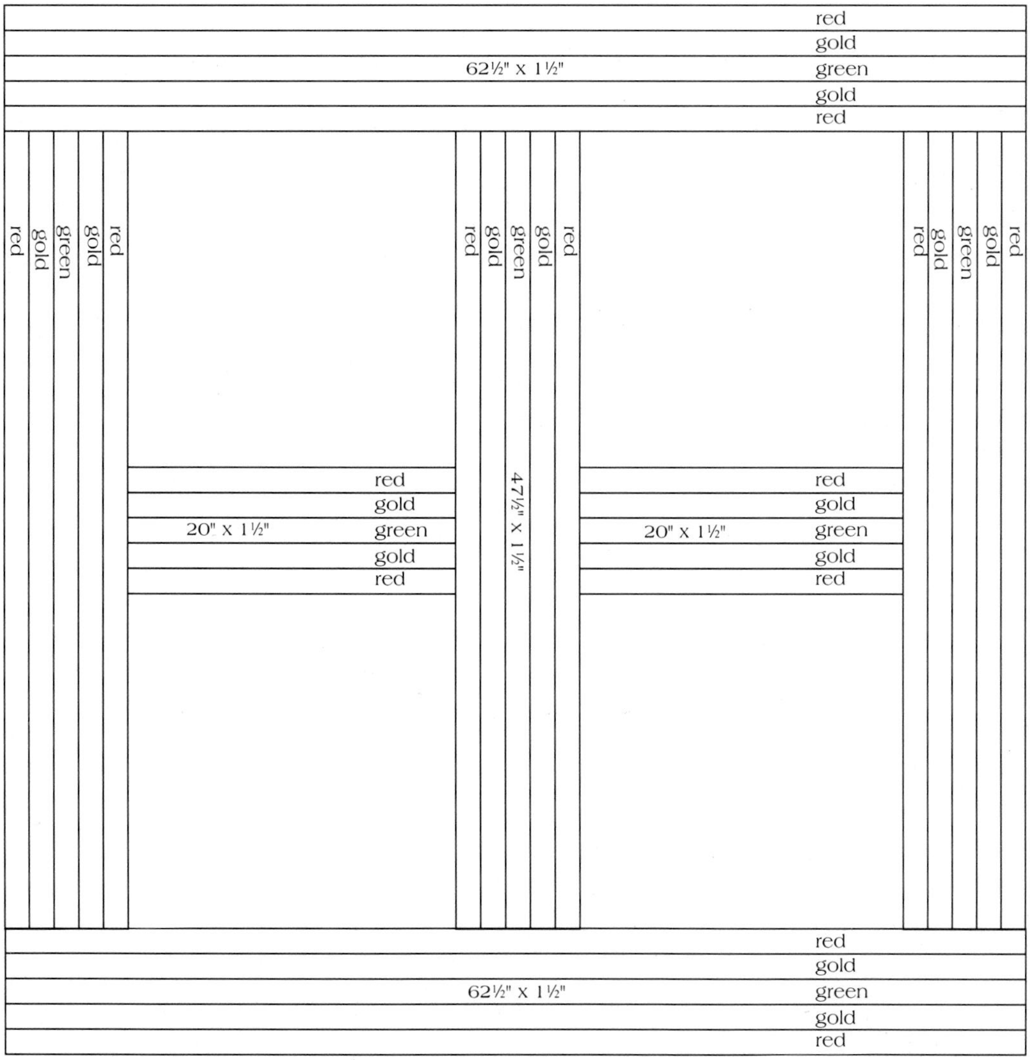

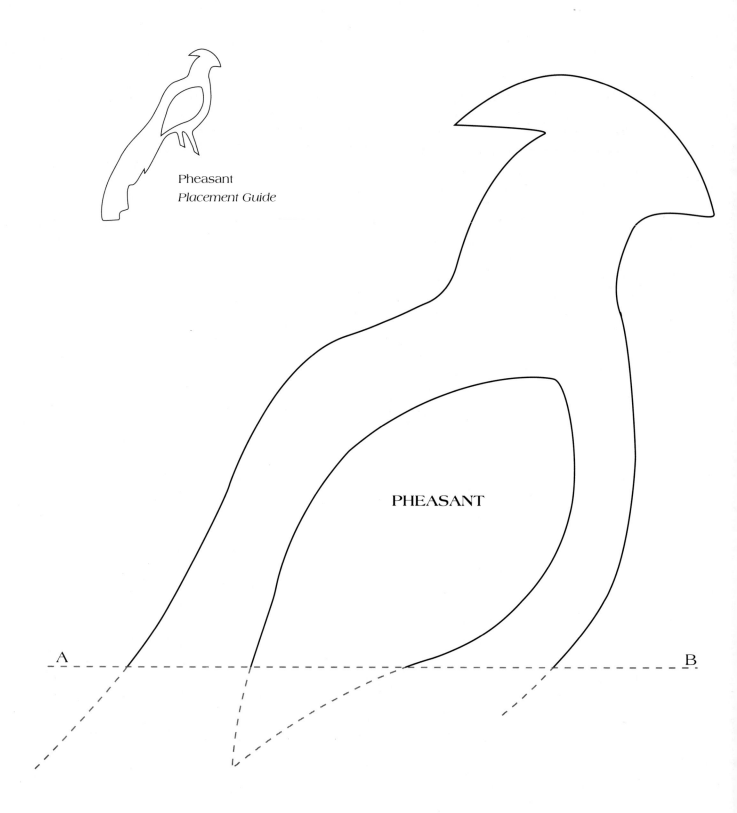

Pheasant
Placement Guide

PHEASANT

A

B

B

A

PHEASANT

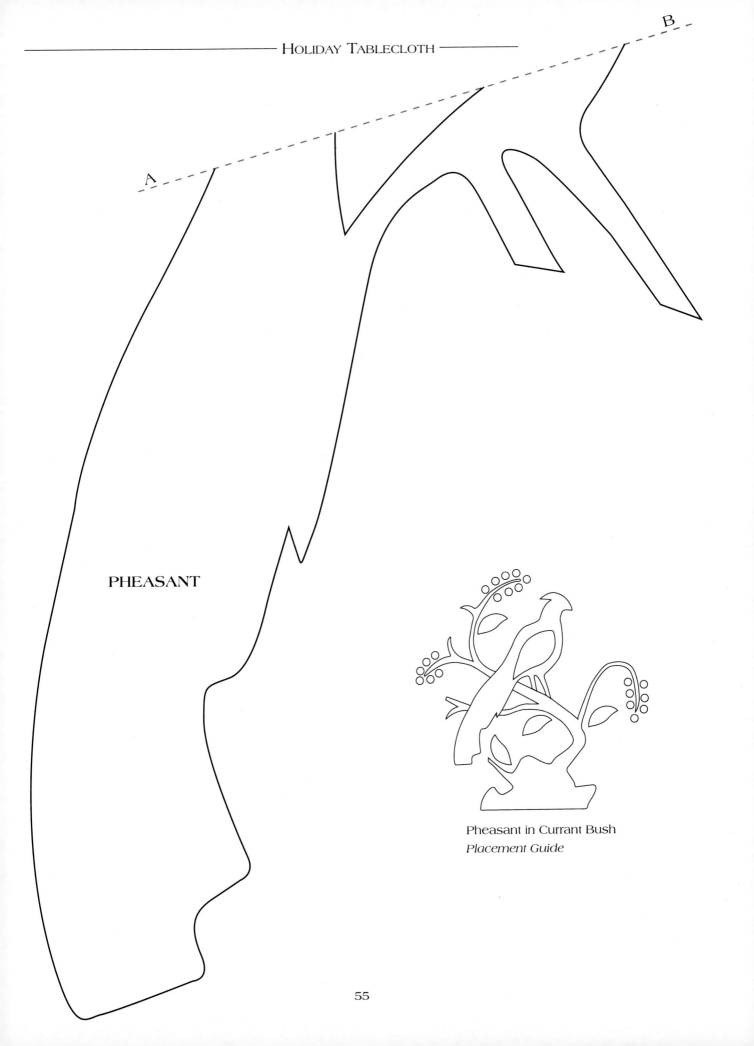

Pheasant in Currant Bush
Placement Guide

Pattern shown on this page is not to scale; pattern shown for placement only. Use full size patterns shown with the Silent Night quilt pages 70-71.

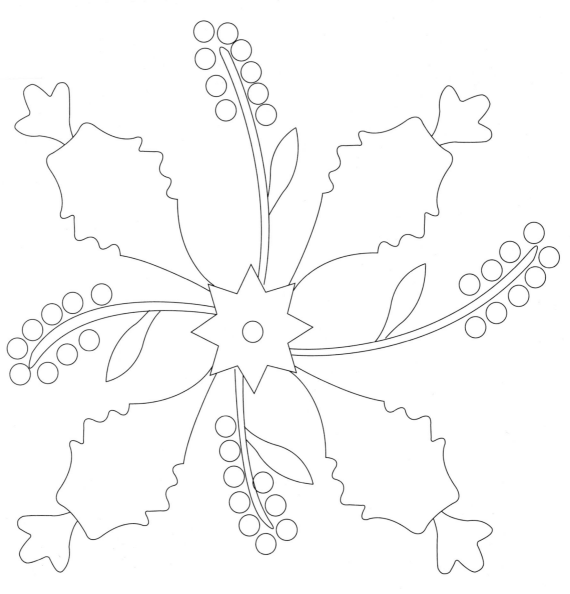

Coxcombs
Placement Guide

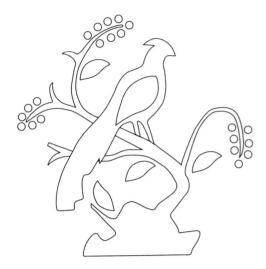

Pheasant in Currant Bush
Placement Guide

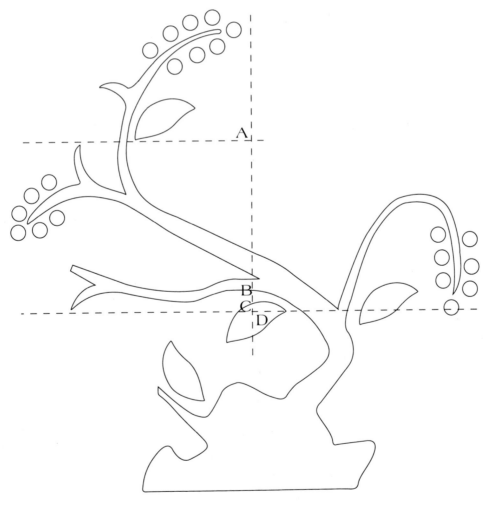

Currant Bush
Placement Guide

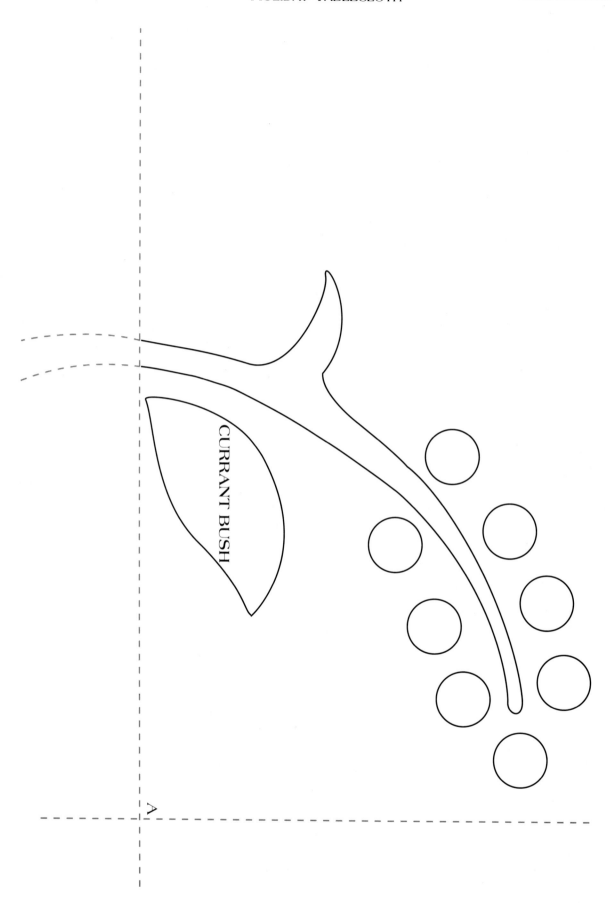

CURRANT BUSH

A

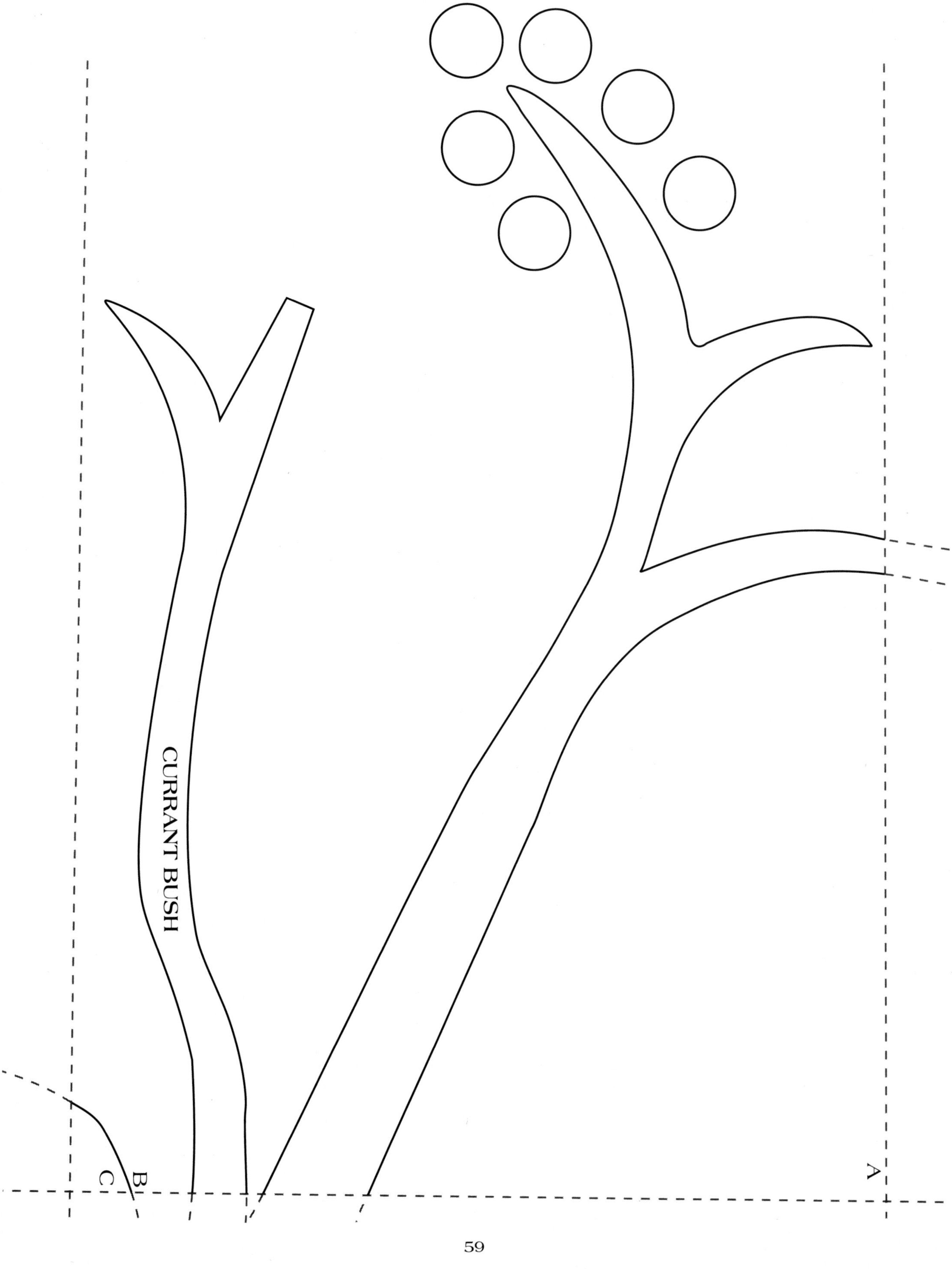

CURRANT BUSH

C

B

A

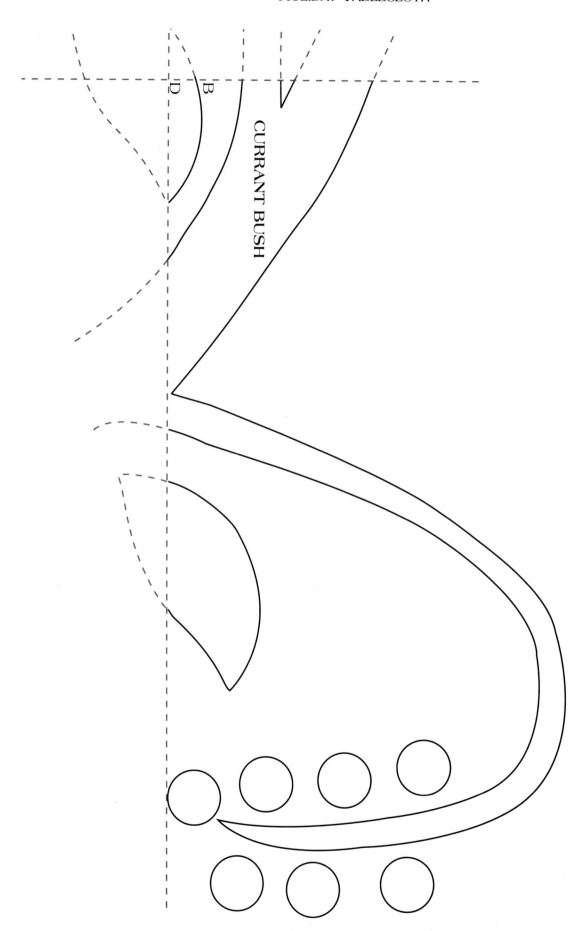

CURRANT BUSH

D B

CURRANT BUSH

C D

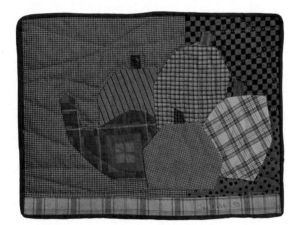

FALL PLACEMATS
17" x 12" finished size

FABRIC REQUIREMENTS
Backgrounds
Fat quarters are great. 3 or 4
cut up will do all three placemats
Otherwise – ⅓ yd.
Pumpkin and squash
¼ yd or fat quarter for each
Scraps for leaves & cat
House – ¼ yd
Roof – ¼ yd
Scraps for windows, chimney,
and door

INSTRUCTIONS (Patterns: pages 142-146, 147, 148-150, 151)

CAT AND LEAF PLACEMAT
- Cut 6½" x 4" (+sa) rectangle
- Cut 6½" x 7" (+sa) rectangle
- Cut 10½" x 11" (+sa) rectangle
- Cut 17" x 1" (+sa) strip
- Piece according to **Diagram #1**
- Cut 1 cat, 1 leaf, and 1 reverse leaf
- Appliqué in place referring to photo

PUMPKIN AND SQUASH PLACEMAT
- Cut 11" x 11" (+sa) square
- Cut 6" x 11" (+sa) rectangle
- Cut 17" x 1" (+sa) strip
- Piece according to **Diagram #2**
- Cut pumpkins and squash
- Appliqué in place referring to photo

HOUSE PLACEMAT
- Cut and piece reverse house
- Appliqué windows and doors in place
- Cut 17" x 2" (+sa) strip
- Sew to bottom of house block

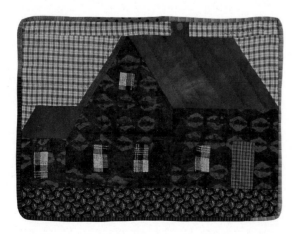

Diagram #1

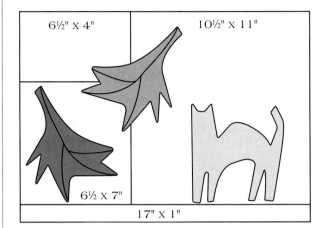

6½" X 4"

10½" X 11"

6½ X 7"

17" X 1"

Diagram #2

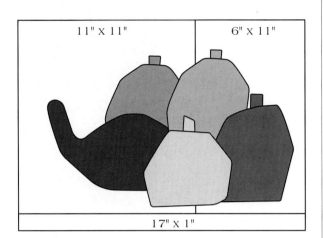

11" X 11"

6" X 11"

17" X 1"

Diagram #3

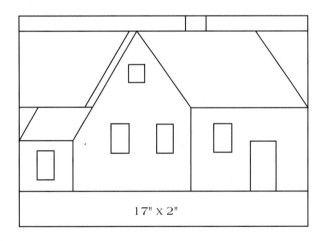

17" X 2"

Page 151

Page 147

Page 148

Page 142

AUTUMN LEAVES
21" x 24½" finished size

FABRIC REQUIREMENTS
   10 – 8" squares of background
      fabric
   Scraps for leaves and geese

INSTRUCTIONS (Pattern: page 151)
- Cut 9 – 7" x 7" (+sa) squares
- Cut 1 – 7" x 3½" (+sa) rectangle
- Cut and piece 2 flying geese blocks according to **Diagram #2**
- Cut 4 leaves and 5 reverse leaves
- Appliqué leaves to 7" x 7" blocks
- Sew blocks together in 3 vertical rows according to **Diagram #1**
- Sew rows together (See **Diagram #1**)

Diagram #1

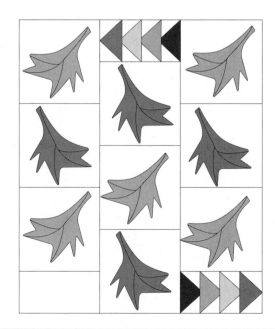

Diagram #2

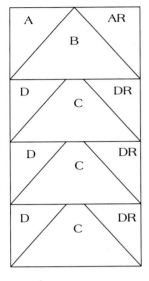

Flying Geese
Placement Guide

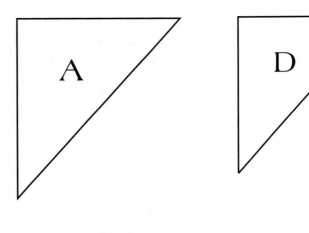

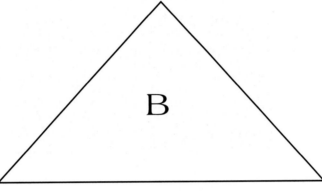

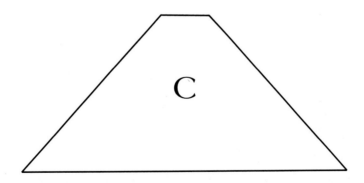

Page 151

SILENT NIGHT
53" x 69" finished size

FABRIC REQUIREMENTS
  Background
    2½ yds total of assorted lights,
    darks, and mediums
  Bias, vines, and leaves
    ½ yd total
    (133" of ¼" (+sa) – 12 – 12" bias strips sewn end to end)
  Large house
    ¼ yd
  Roof
    ¼ yd
  Scraps for windows, doors
  Scraps for other buildings and
    trees
  Borders
    1⅛ yd of dark

INSTRUCTIONS (Patterns: pages 69-79)
- Piece background according to **Diagram #1**
- Cut and piece 133" of ¼" (+sa) bias stripping. 12 – 12" strips sewn end to end will make your bias.
- Cut out Coxcombs and Star pieces (See **Diagram #2**)
- Appliqué Coxcombs and Star, bias and berries onto background referring to the photo.
- Cut out church, roofs, steeple, door, and windows
- Appliqué roof to steeple, windows, door, and steeple to church
- Appliqué church to background referring to photo
- Cut 3 large trees and 7 small trees
- Appliqué trees to background referring to photo
- Cut 2 – 63" x 5" (+sa) borders
- Sew 63" x 5" borders to sides
- Cut 2 – 53" x 5" (+sa) borders
- Sew 53" x 5" borders to top and bottom
- Cut out and appliqué town for upper right corner. This consists of house "E," house "C," and a school building. The buildings overlap. Referring to photo, sew buildings together as a group and then appliqué to quilt. (In my quilts this was Lexington, MO where Max was in military school. In your quilt it can be wherever you wish. This applies to the next two towns also.)
- Cut out and appliqué in two rows town in lower right corner.
  This town consists of :
  > Back row – Bldg. A, Bldg. D
  > Front row – Bldg. C, Bldg. B, Bldg. E.

  The buildings overlap. Referring to the photo, sew the buildings together as a group and then appliqué to quilt (Kansas City, MO, where my mother lives for me, wherever for you).
- Cut out and appliqué school building in lower left corner referring to photo for placement (Missouri Western outside of St. Joseph, MO where Kelly and Brian were in school).

Diagram #1

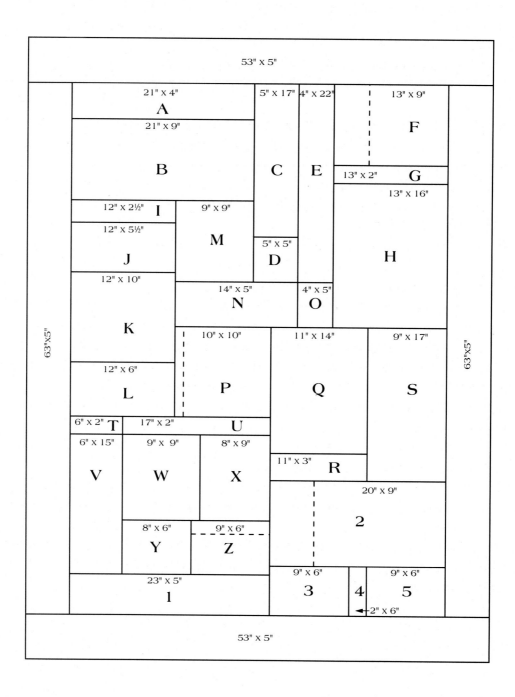

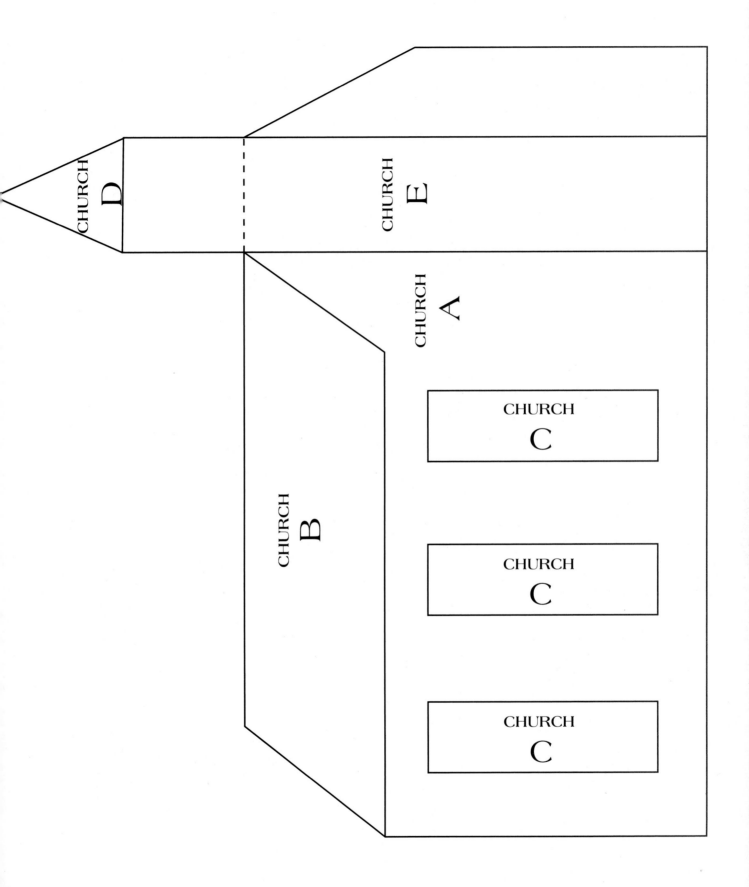

Diagram #2

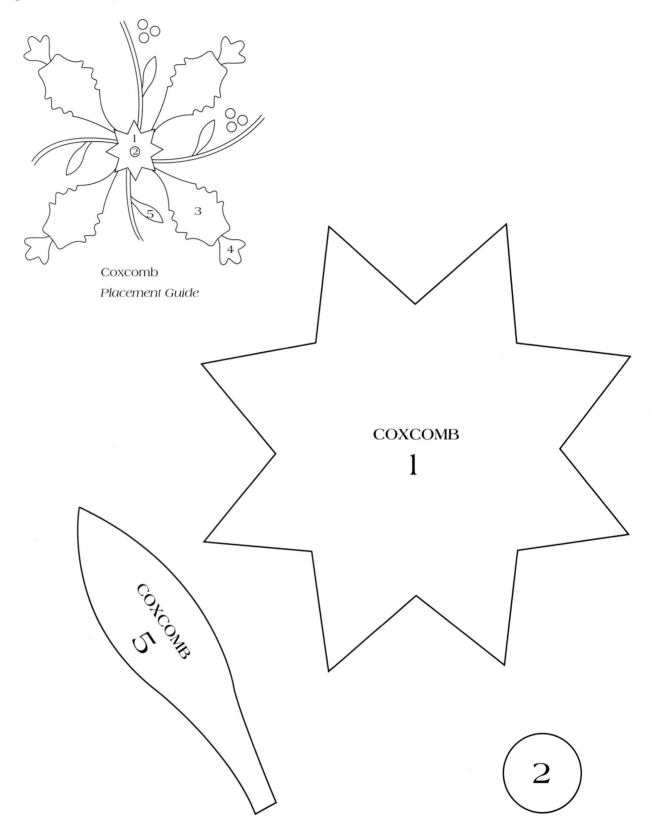

Coxcomb
Placement Guide

COXCOMB
1

COXCOMB 5

2

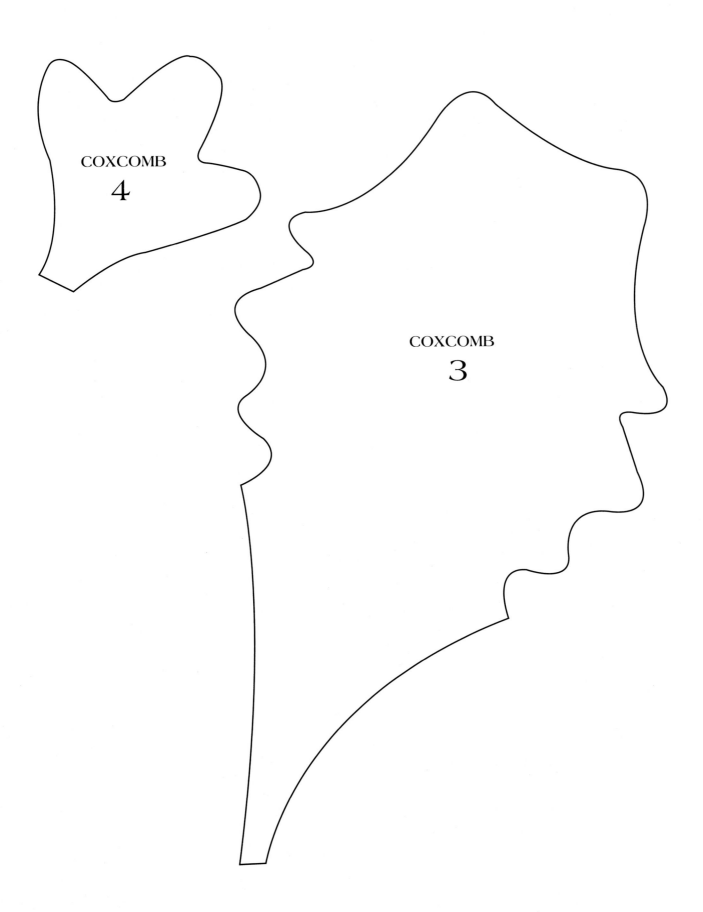

COXCOMB
4

COXCOMB
3

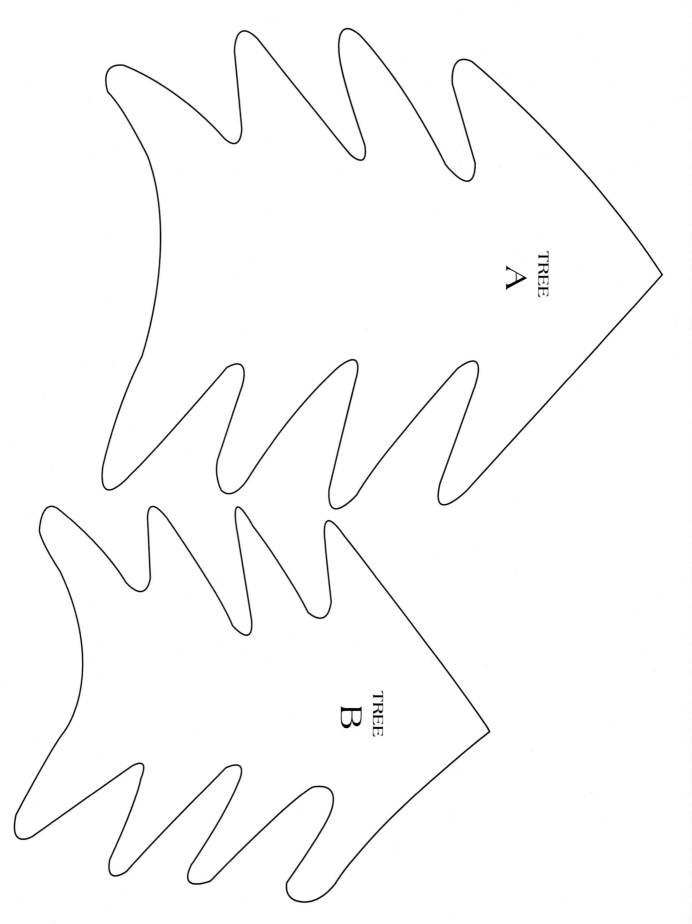

TREE A

TREE B

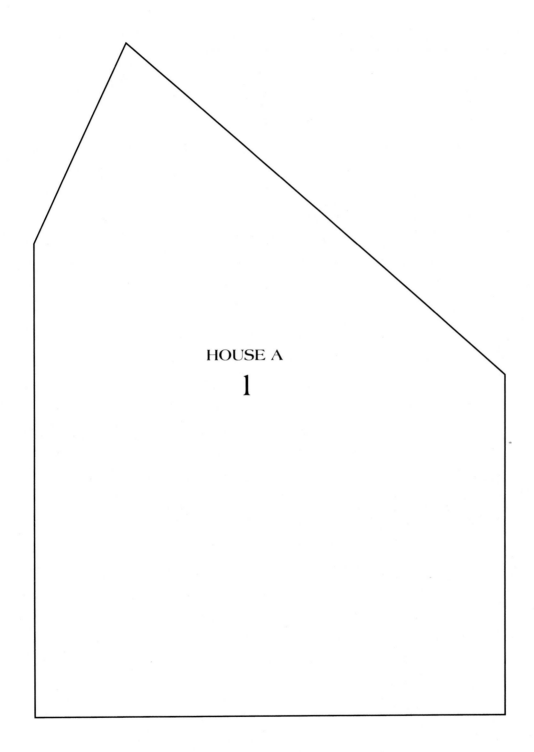

HOUSE A
1

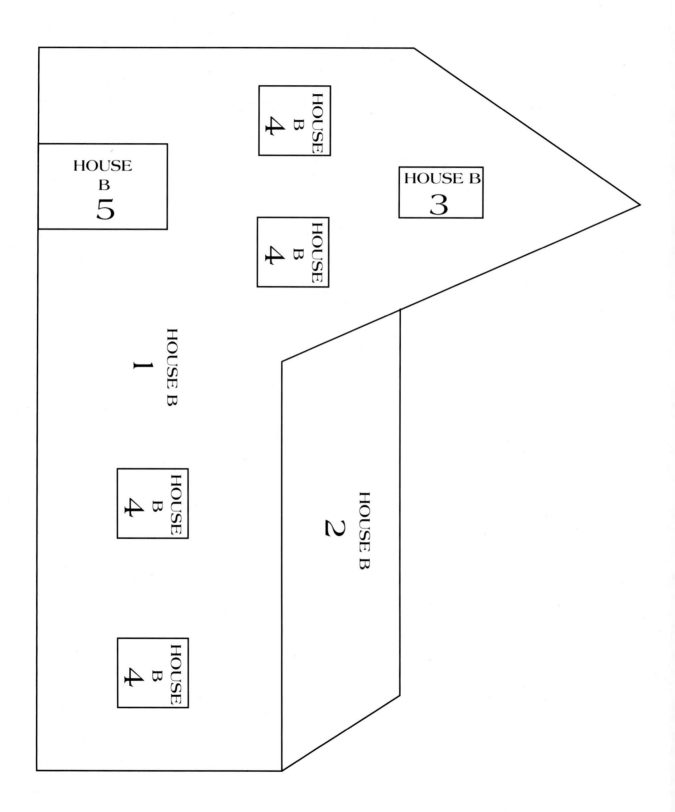

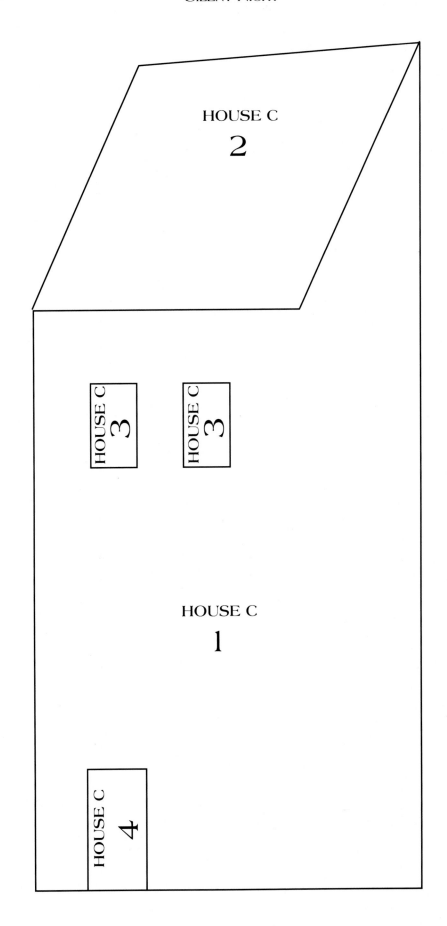

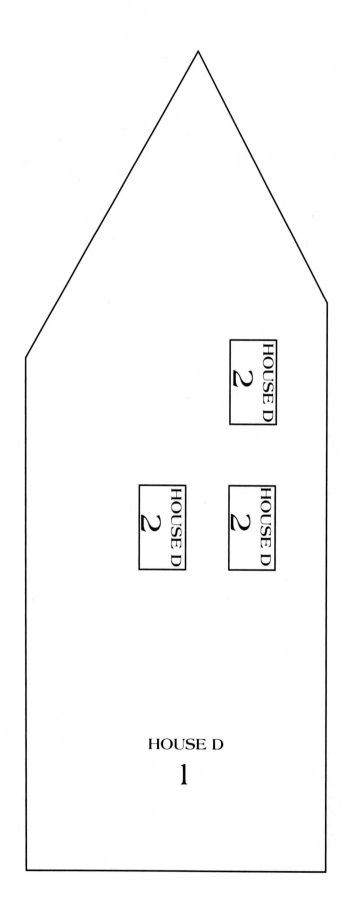

HOUSE D

1

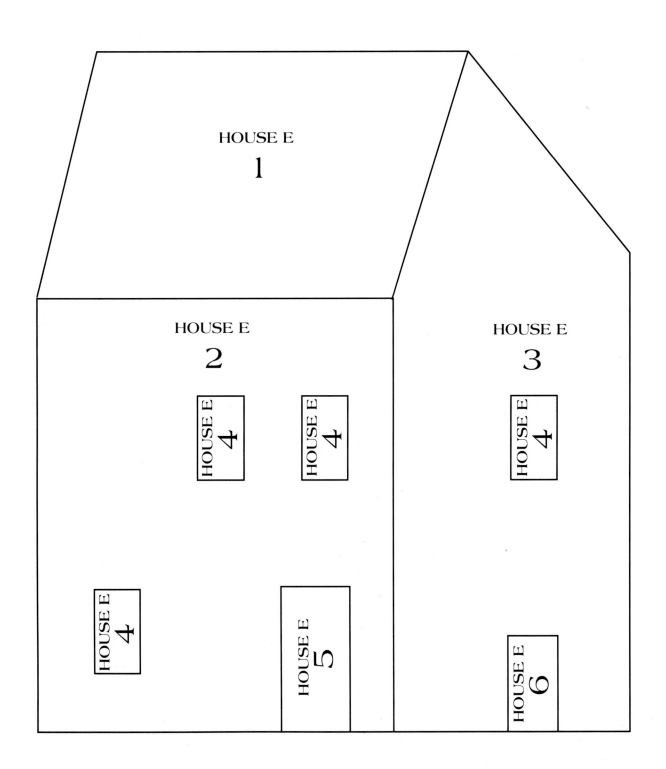

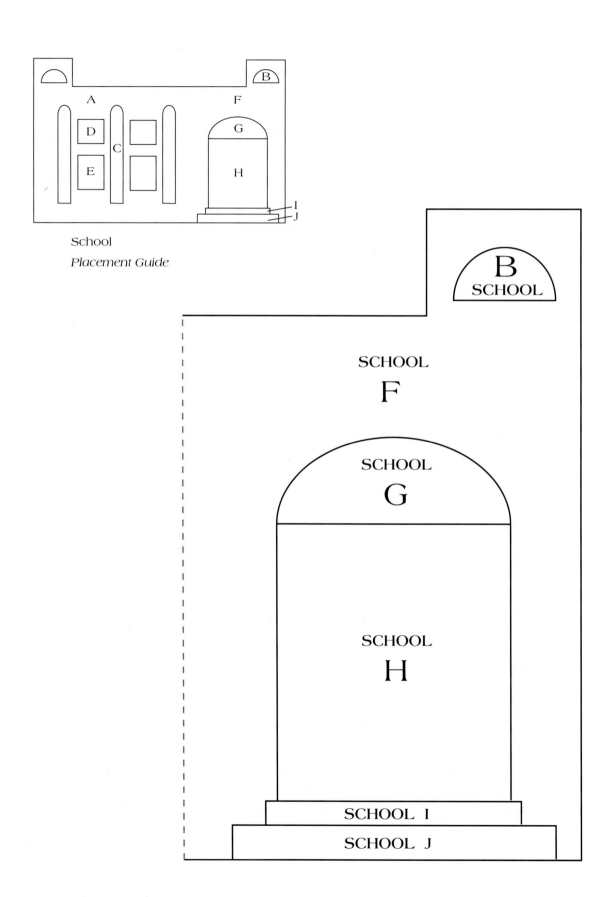

School

Placement Guide

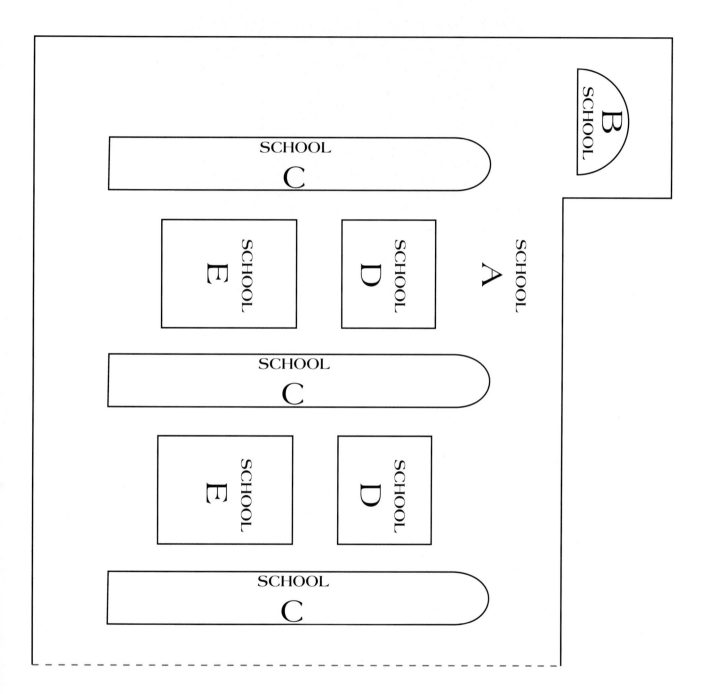

SANTA TABLE RUNNER

44" x 30" finished size

FABRIC REQUIREMENTS
  Background
    ⅝ yd
  Reindeer
    ¼ yd or fat quarter
  Scraps for Santa, trees, stars, and
    snowman
  Borders
    ¼ yd for inner border
    ⅓ yd for outer border

INSTRUCTIONS (Patterns: pages 82-83, 153, 154, 155, 158)
  • Cut background rectangle 34" x 20" (+sa)
  • Cut 7½" x 7½" square
  • Appliqué tree to square
  • Appliqué beard to Santa. (This is a smaller Santa than the one in the placemats
    and wallhanging.)
  • Appliqué tree block, Santa, Santa's bag, two trees (these are smaller trees also),
    snowman, reindeer, and two stars onto background according to the photo.
  • Cut 2 – 34" x 1" (+sa) inner borders

- Cut 2 – 22" x 1" (+sa) inner borders
- Sew 34" x 1" borders to top and bottom
- Sew 22" x 1" borders to sides
- Cut 2 – 22" x 4" (+sa) outer borders
- Cut 2 – 44" x 4" (+sa) outer borders
- Sew 22" x 4" borders to sides
- Sew 44" x 4" borders to top and bottom
- Appliqué remaining star in place according to photo.

Background Diagram

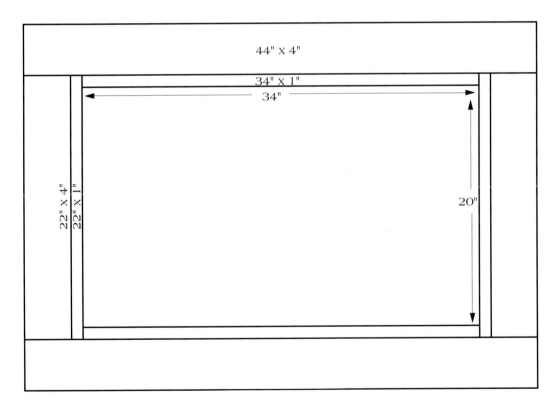

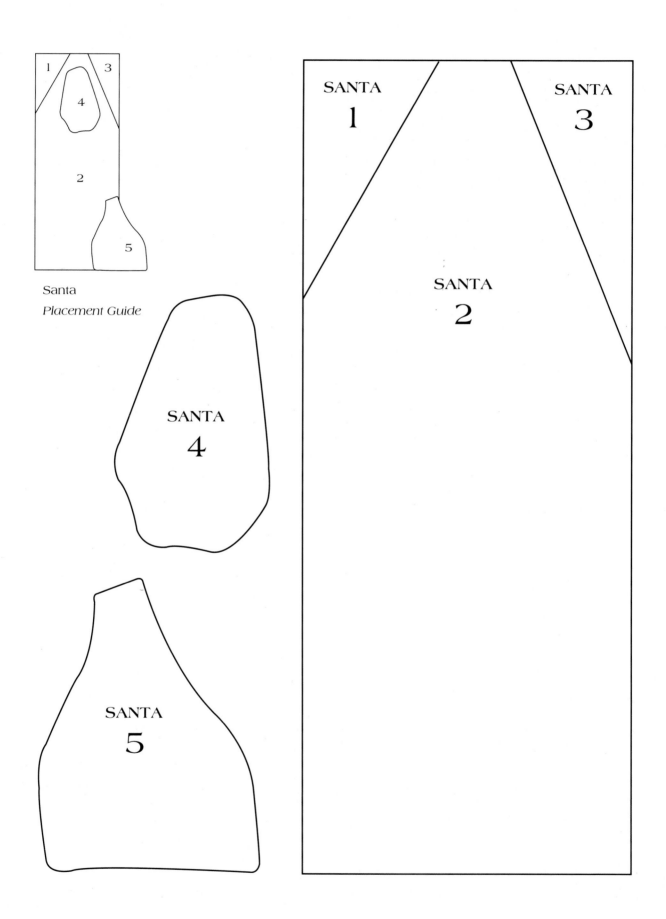

Santa

Placement Guide

SANTA
1

SANTA
3

SANTA
2

SANTA
4

SANTA
5

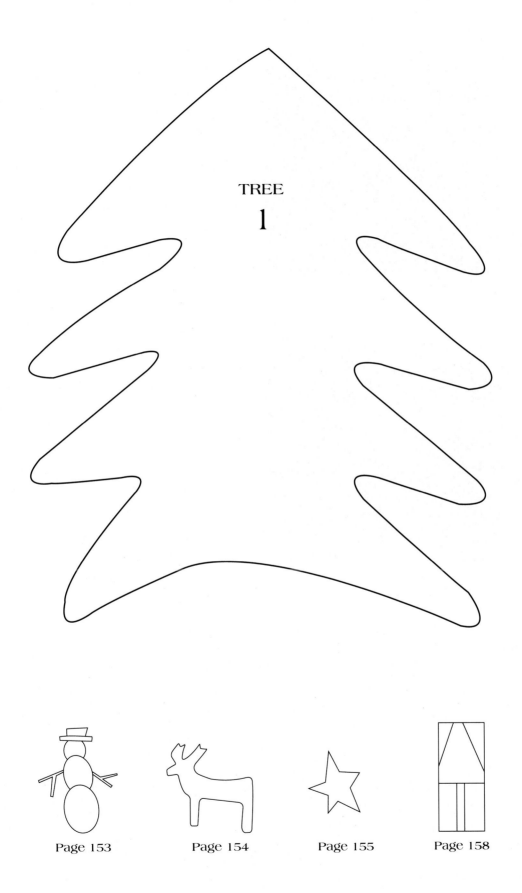

TREE
1

Page 153   Page 154   Page 155   Page 158

SANTA PLACEMATS
15" x 17" finished size

FABRIC REQUIREMENTS
(Yardage given is for one placemat)

Background
¼ yd total of lights
Reindeer
Fat quarter or ¼ yd
Santa and Trees
⅛ yd each or scraps
Scrap for star
Borders
⅛ yd for inner border
¼ yd for outer border
(½ yd for all three)

INSTRUCTIONS (Patterns: pages 87, 152, 154, 156)

SANTA, REINDEER, STAR
- Cut and piece Santa block and star block.
- Cut 10" x 4" (+sa) rectangle. Sew to right of Santa block.
- Cut 6" x 4" (+sa) rectangle. Sew to bottom of star, making a 10" x 4" (+sa) rectangle. Sew to right of blank rectangle. (Santa, blank rectangle, star rectangle)
- Appliqué Santa's beard, bag, and reindeer in place according to the photo.

SANTA, TWO TREES
- Cut and piece Santa block
- Cut and piece 2 tree blocks
- Assemble in following order: Santa, tree, tree
- Appliqué Santa's beard and bag in place

SANTA, REINDEER, TREE

- Cut and piece Santa block
- Cut 10" x 4" rectangle
- Cut and piece tree block
- Assemble in the following order: Santa, rectangle, tree
- Appliqué Santa's beard and bag in place
- Follow general instructions (below) for borders
- Appliqué reindeer in place according to photo

GENERAL INSTRUCTIONS

- Cut 2 – 12" x ½" (+sa) inner borders
- Cut 2 – 11" x ½" (+sa) inner borders
- Sew 12" x ½" borders to the top and bottom
- Sew 11" x ½" borders to the sides
- Cut 2 – 11" x 2" (+sa) outer borders
- Cut 2 – 17" x 2" (+sa) outer borders
- Sew 11" x 2" borders to the sides
- Sew 17" x 2" borders to the top and bottom
- Finish off as placemats

Placemat Diagrams

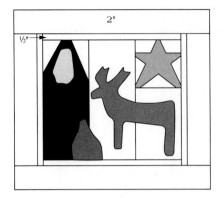

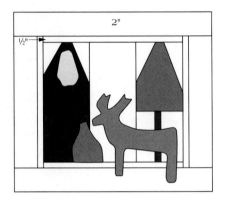

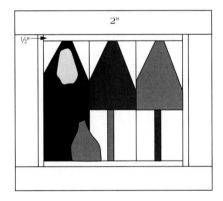

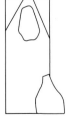

Page 156

Page 154

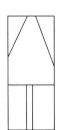

Page 152

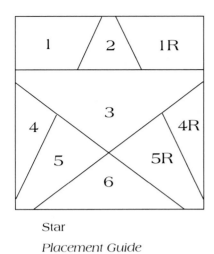

Star

Placement Guide

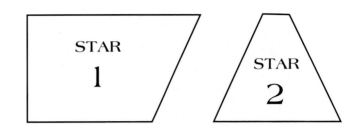

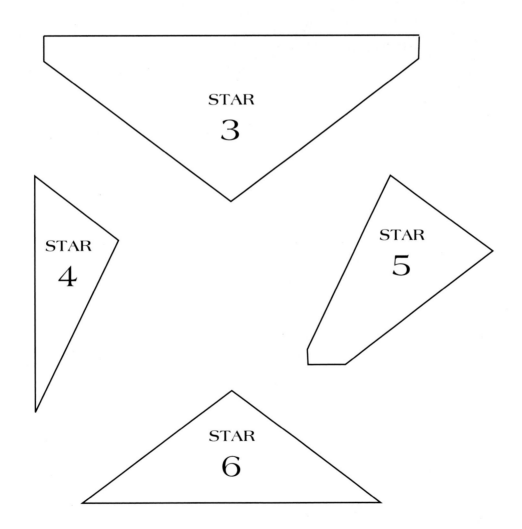

SANTA WALLHANGING
26" x 36" finished size

FABRIC REQUIREMENTS
This is mainly a "scrap" quilt except for the borders. If you are buying the material, ⅛ yd will be sufficient whenever the term "scrap" is used, unless otherwise stated.

Scraps for each Santa block, tree block and their backgrounds

Reindeer
 Fat quarter or scrap ¼ yd wide

Reindeer Background
 Fat quarter or scrap ¼ yd wide
 ¼ yd total will do for all three backgrounds if you wish to make them of the same material.

Borders
 ⅛ yd for inner border
 ¼ yd for middle border
 ⅛ yd for outer border

INSTRUCTIONS (Patterns: pages 152, 154, 156)
- Cut and piece 3 Santa blocks
- Cut and piece 6 tree blocks
- Cut 3 – 8" x 10" (+sa) rectangles
- Cut 2 reindeer and 1 reverse reindeer
- Appliqué a reindeer to each rectangle
- Assemble Santa blocks, tree blocks, and reindeer blocks into three horizontal rows according to the **Diagram #1**
- Cut 2 – 20" x ½" (+sa) inner borders
- Cut 2 – 30" x ½" (+sa) inner borders
- Sew 20" x ½" borders to top and bottom
- Sew 30" x ½" borders to sides
- Cut 2 – 30" x 2" (+sa) middle borders
- Cut 2 – 26" x 2" (+sa) middle borders

- Sew 30" x 2" borders to sides
- Sew 26" x 2" borders to top and bottom
- Cut 2 – 26" x ½" (+sa) outer borders
- Cut 2 – 35" x ½" (+sa) outer borders
- Sew 26" x ½" borders to top and bottom
- Sew 35½" x ½" borders to sides

Diagram #1

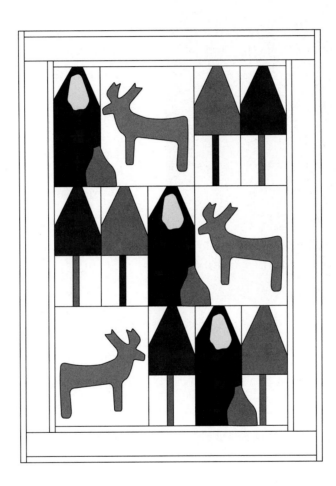

Page 156

Page 154

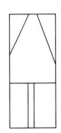

Page 152

SNOWFLAKES & CEDARS
59" x 84" finished size

FABRIC REQUIREMENTS
House
   ¼ yd
Roof
   ¼ yd
Scraps for windows and door
Scraps for trees
Hexagons
   1 ¼ yd of mediums
Stars
   1 ⅓ yd of darks for triangle points
House and trees background
   1 yd total of assorted darks and
      mediums
Borders
   1 ⅓ yd of darks for side and
      bottom borders
   ½ yd of medium for top border
      and sky above hexagons
Binding
   ¼ yd for straight binding

INSTRUCTIONS (Patterns: pages 92-93, 96-97, 142-146)
- Piece 6 log cabin type diamonds according to **Diagram #1**. This is pieced more like a courthouse steps block. Sew both B's to A, then both C's, then both D's, etc. Also B & C are the same color, D & E, and F & G.
- Cut 68 dark triangle points for the stars – piece H.
- Cut 36 medium hexagons
- Sew log cabin diamonds, triangles, and hexagons into 6 vertical rows as seen in **Diagram #2**. Sew these rows together as seen in **Diagram #4**.
- Cut and piece background for house and trees as seen in **Diagram #3**. You will use both piecing and appliqué for the background.
- Cut 5 small trees, 2 large trees, and a house with roof, windows, door and chimney.

- Appliqué roof, chimney, door, and windows to house
- Appliqué house and trees to background
- Appliqué background to rows of hexagons
- Cut 45" x 6" (+sa) strip for sky
- Appliqué rows of hexagons to sky with hexagons in rows 2, 4, & 6 touching seam allowance line
- Cut 45" x 4½" (+sa) dark border
- Sew 45" x 4½" border to bottom
- Cut 2 – 80" x 7" (+sa) borders
- Sew 80" x 7" borders to side
- Cut 59" x 4" (+sa) border of "sky" material
- Sew 59" x 4" border to top
- Quilt and bind.

Thanks to Gerry Kimmel for the idea of the log cabin diamond.

Diagram #1

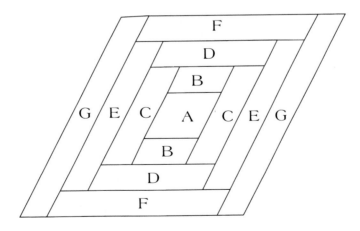

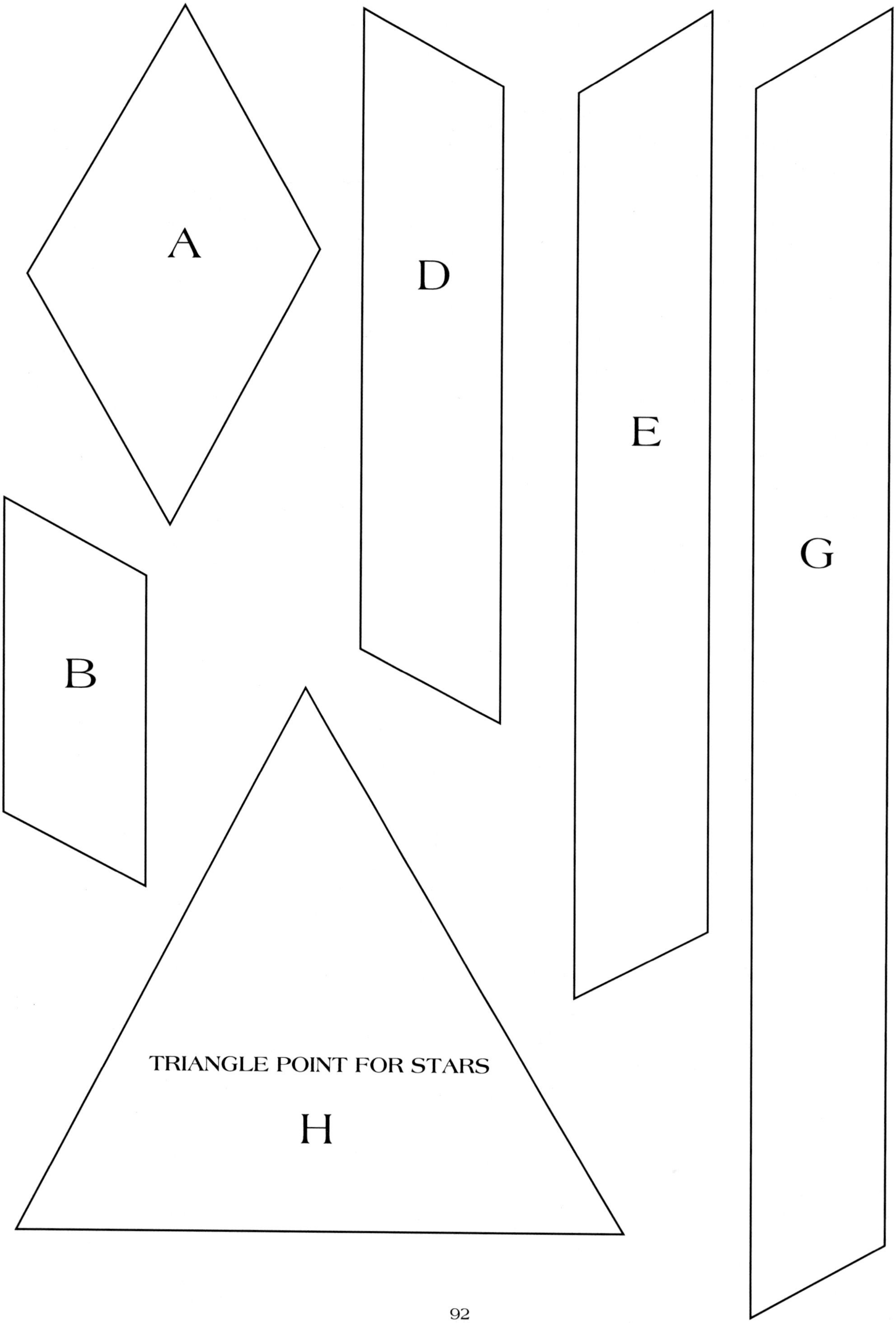

A

D

E

G

B

TRIANGLE POINT FOR STARS

H

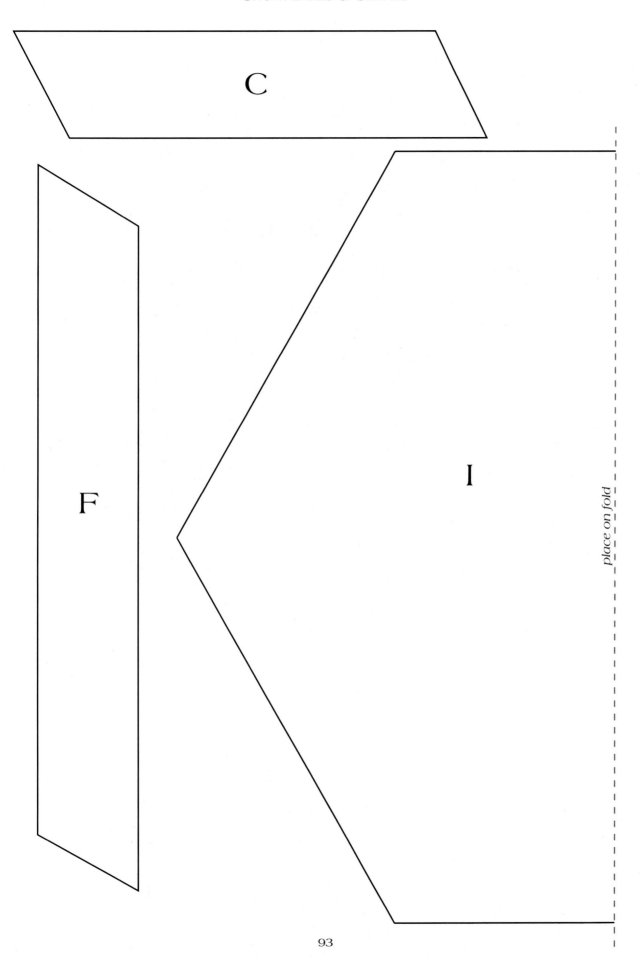

C

F

I

place on fold

Diagram #2

Diagram #3

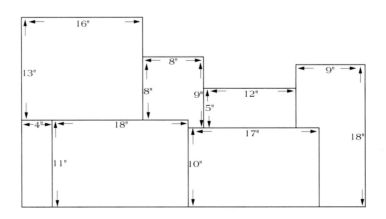

Diagram #4

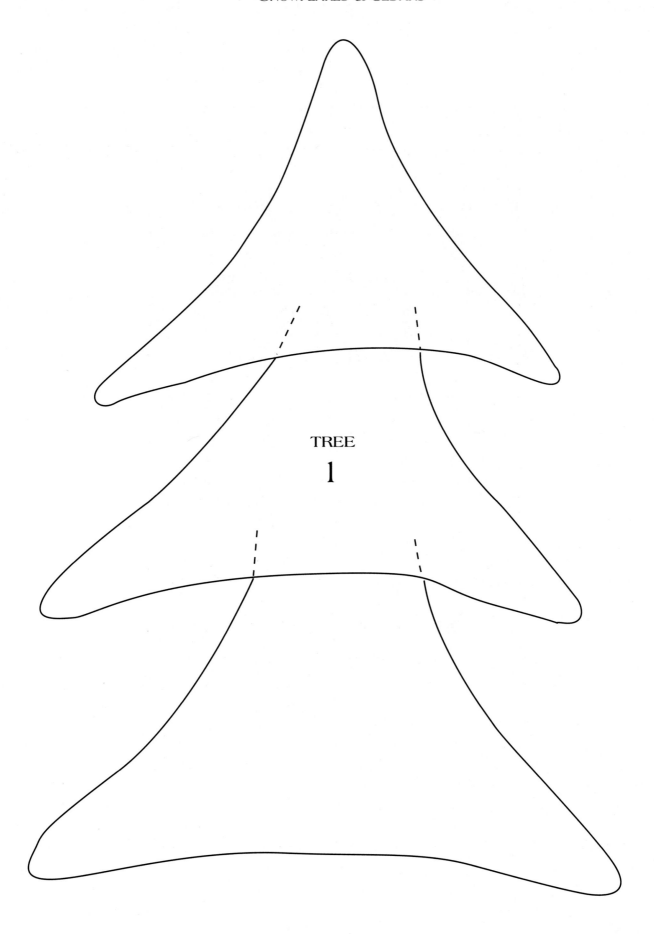

TREE

1

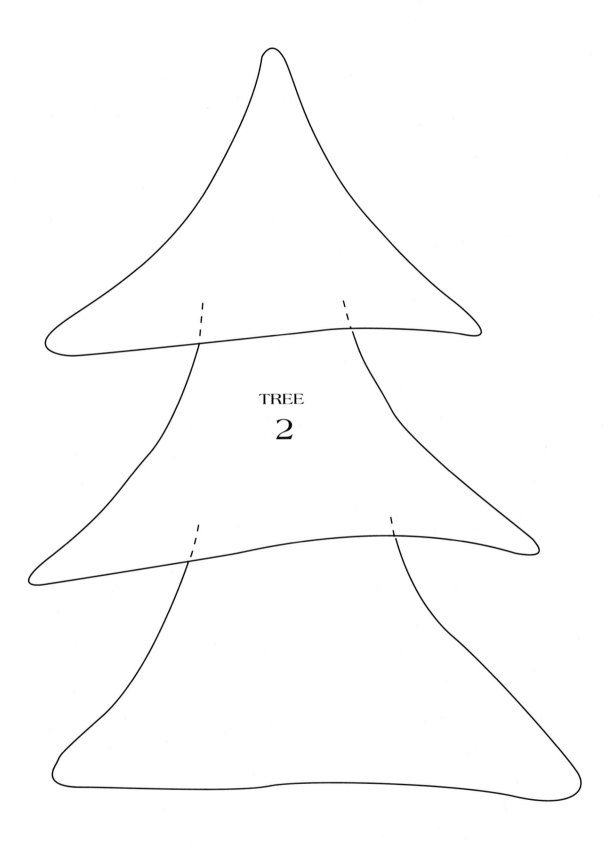

TREE
2

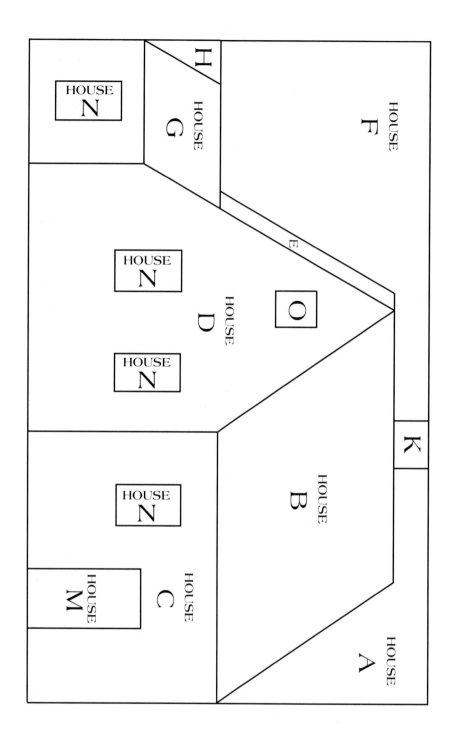

Pattern shown on this page is not to scale; pattern shown for placement only. Use the full size pattern, in reverse, shown in the Additional Pattern Section, page 142.

Full Quilt Diagram

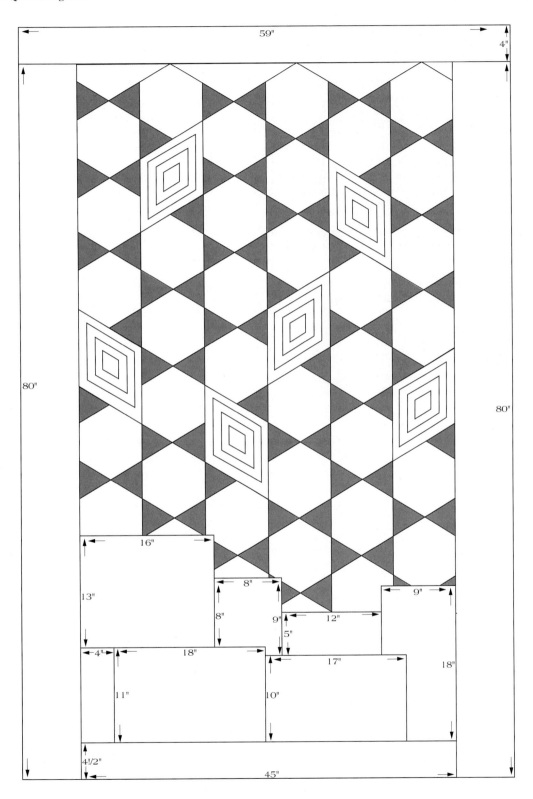

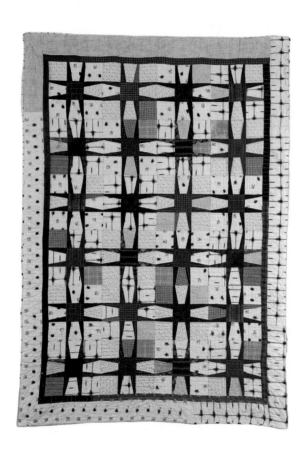

WINTER SOLSTICE
60" x 84" finished size

FABRIC REQUIREMENTS
Background
2¾ yd total of lights (with scraps
of mediums thrown in)
Blocks
1¾ yd total darks for blocks
Borders
½ yd total darks for inner border
1⅛ yd total lights for outer border
Binding
¼ yd for straight binding

INSTRUCTIONS (Pattern: page 102)
- Cut and piece 24 Winter Solstice blocks
- Sew six rows of four blocks each
- Sew together rows
- Cut 2 – 72½" x 1½" (+sa) inner borders
- Cut 2 – 51" x 1½" (+sa) inner borders
- Sew 72½" x 1½" borders to sides
- Sew 51" x 1½" borders to top and bottom
- Cut 2 – 51" x 4½" (+sa) outer borders
- Cut 2 – 84" x 4½" (+sa) outer borders
- Sew 51" x 4½" borders to top and bottom
- Sew 84" x 4½" borders to sides
- Borders may be pieced if you wish

Full Quilt Diagram

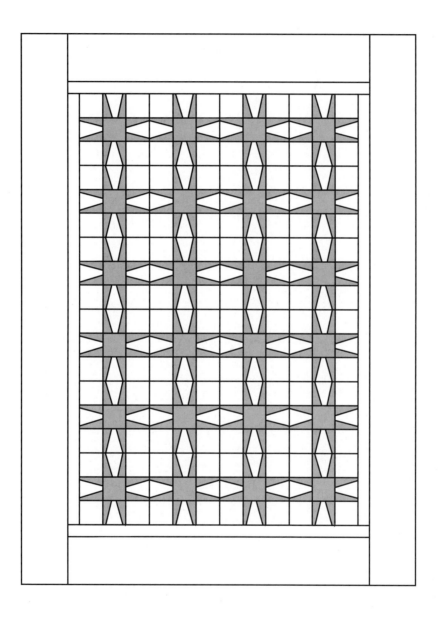

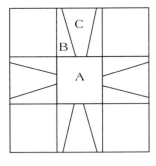

Winter Solstice Block

Placement Guide

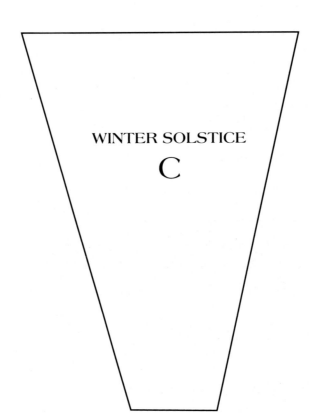

WINTER SOLSTICE

C

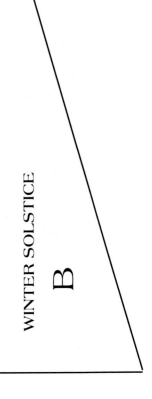

WINTER SOLSTICE

B

WINTER SOLSTICE

A

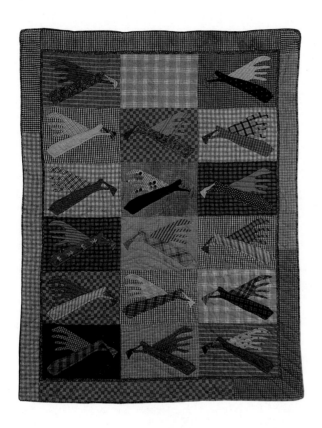

SERAPHIM (Angels)
43" x 55" finished size

FABRIC REQUIREMENTS
  Background
    1 ½ yd total or
      18 – 8 ½" x 12" blocks
  Borders
    ⅛ yd for inner border
    ⅔ yd total lights for outer border
  Binding
    ¼ yd for straight binding

INSTRUCTIONS (Pattern: page 157)
  • Cut 18 – 12" x 8" (+sa) background blocks
  • Cut 8 angels, wings, and horns and 9 reverse angels, wings, and horns
  • Appliqué angels and reverse angels (wings and horns also) to blocks (there will be one blank block)
  • Sew blocks together in six rows of three blocks each according to **Diagram #1**
  • Cut 2 – 48" x ½" (+sa) inner borders
  • Cut 2 – 37" x ½" (+sa) inner borders
  • Sew 48" x ½" borders to sides
  • Sew 37" x ½" borders to top and bottom
  • Cut 2 – 37" x 3" (+sa) outer borders
  • Cut 2 – 55" x 3" (+sa) outer borders
  • Sew 37" x 3" borders to top and bottom
  • Sew 55" x 3" borders to sides
  • Quilt and bind.

Diagram #1

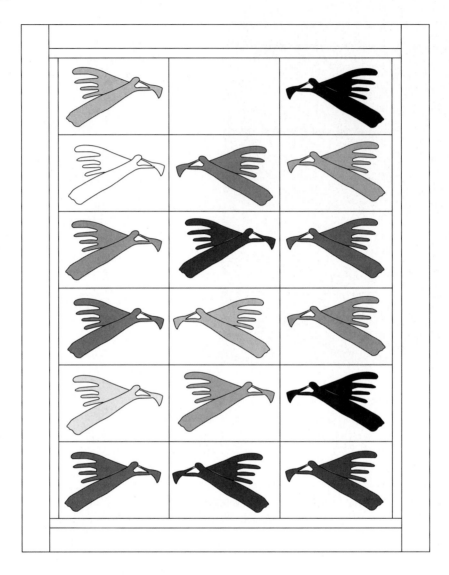

Page 157

SERAPH (Angel)
21" x 14" finished size

FABRIC REQUIREMENTS
Background
  ½ yd
Scraps for angel and horn
Wing
  ¼ yd or fat quarter
Border
  ⅛ yd

INSTRUCTIONS (Patterns pages 106-107)
- Cut background block 19" x 12" (+sa)
- Appliqué wing, horn, and angel according to photo
- Cut 2 – 19" x 1" (+sa) borders
- Cut 2 – 14" x 1" (+sa) borders
- Sew 19" x 1" borders to top and bottom
- Sew 14" x 1" borders to sides
- Quilt and bind.

Full Quilt Diagram

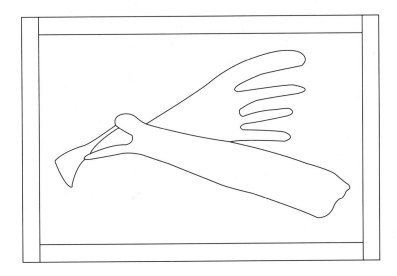

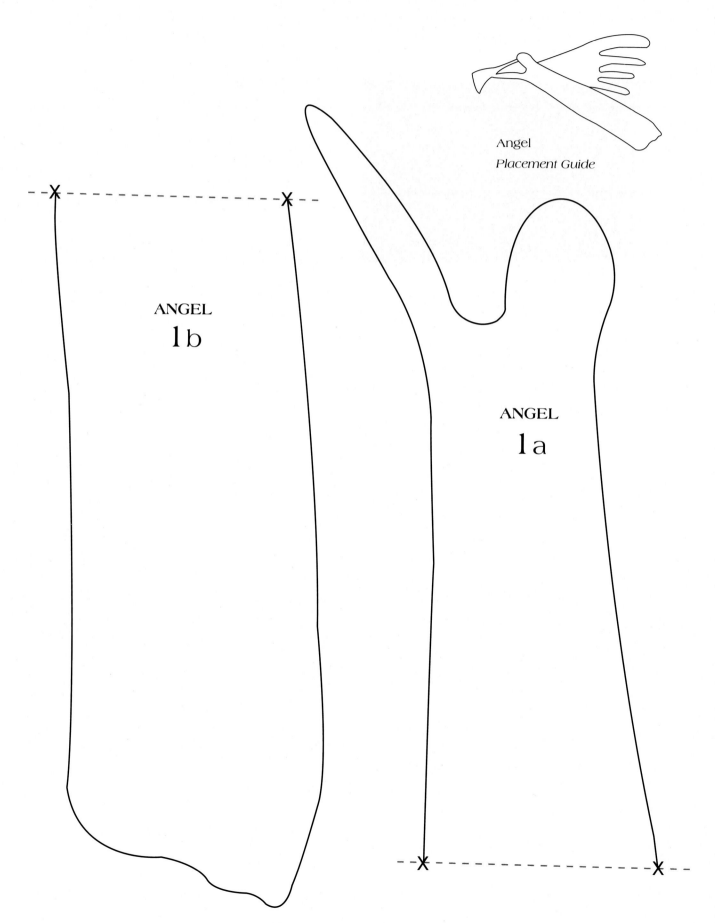

Angel
Placement Guide

ANGEL
1b

ANGEL
1a

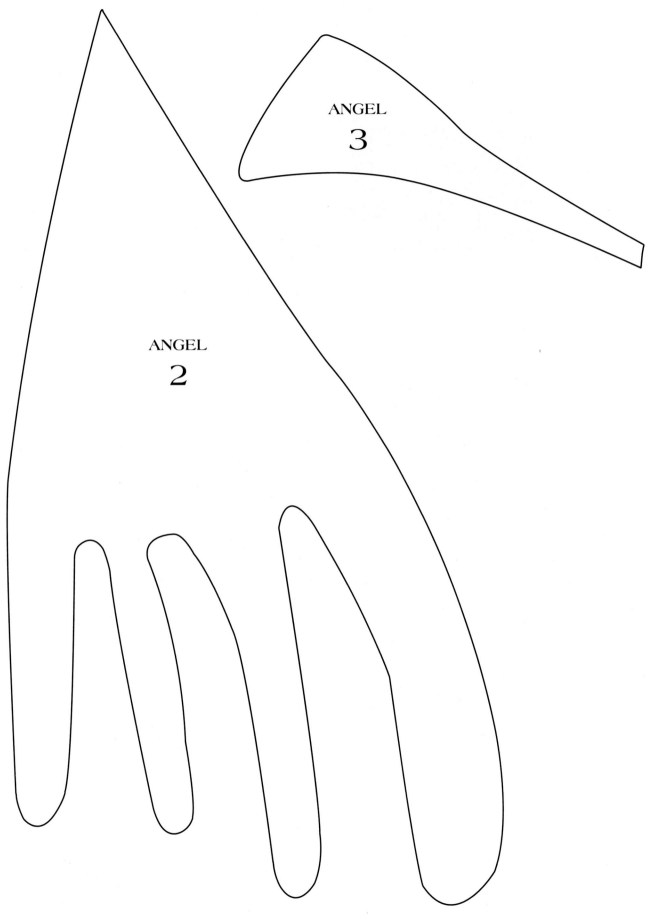

ANGEL
3

ANGEL
2

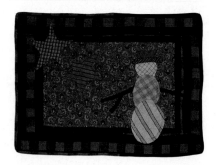

SNOWMAN PLACEMAT
18" x 13" finished size

FABRIC REQUIREMENTS
Background
 ¼ yd for background
Borders
 ⅛ yd for inner border
 ¼ yd for outer border
Scraps for snowman and stars

INSTRUCTIONS (Patterns: pages 153, 155)
- Cut background block 12½" x 7½" (+sa)
- Cut 2 – 12½" x ¾" (+sa) inner borders
- Cut 2 – 9" x ¾" (+sa) inner borders
- Sew 12½" x ¾" borders to top and bottom
- Sew 9" x ¾" borders to sides
- Cut 2 – 9" x 2" (+sa) outer borders
- Cut 2 – 18" x 2" (+sa) outer borders
- Sew 9" x 2" borders to sides
- Sew 18" x 2" borders to top and bottom
- Appliqué snowman and stars in place referring to photo.
- Quilt and bind.

Background Diagram

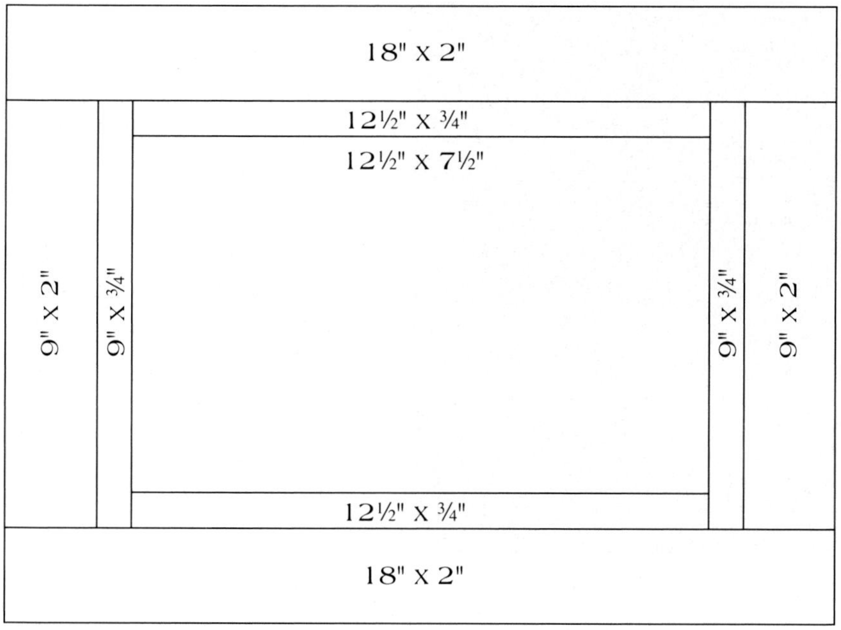

18" X 2"	
12½" X ¾"	
12½" X 7½"	
9" X 2" 9" X ¾"	9" X ¾" 9" X 2"
12½" X ¾"	
18" X 2"	

Page 153

Page 155

SNOWMAN WALLHANGING
19" x 27" finished size

FABRIC REQUIREMENTS
  Background
    ¼ yd of 4 different backgrounds
  Scraps for snowman
  Borders
    ⅛ yd for inner border
    ¼ yd for outer border

INSTRUCTIONS (Pattern: page 153)
  • Cut 4 background blocks 8" x 12" (+sa)
  • Appliqué a snowman to each block leaving an opening on each side of the snowman for a twig arm. (Or make cloth arms if you wish.)
  • Sew the four blocks together.
  • Cut 2 – 16" x ½" (+sa) borders
  • Cut 2 – 25" x ½" (+sa) borders
  • Sew 16" x ½" borders to top and bottom
  • Sew 25" x ½" borders to the sides
  • Cut 2 – 25" x 1" (+sa) borders
  • Cut 2 – 19" x 1" (+sa) borders
  • Sew 25" x 1" borders to the sides
  • Sew 19" x 1" borders to the top and bottom
  • Quilt and bind
  • When quilting is finished, sew on button eyes and buttons down the front of each snowman. Then slip twigs into opening on snowmen and whipstitch into place.

Background Diagram

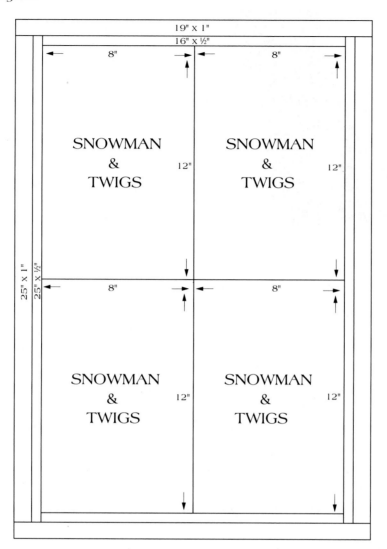

19" x 1"

16" x ½"

8"

8"

SNOWMAN
&
TWIGS

12"

SNOWMAN
&
TWIGS

12"

25" x 1"

25" x ½"

8"

8"

SNOWMAN
&
TWIGS

12"

SNOWMAN
&
TWIGS

12"

Page 153

SNOWMAN STOCKING
17½" x 22" finished size

FABRIC REQUIREMENTS
Lining
½ yd
Back
½ yd
Scraps of 8 different materials
for strip piecing
Scrap for toe
Scraps for snowman and stars

INSTRUCTIONS (Patterns pages 114-117, 153, 155)
- Strip piece background approximately 18" x 24"
- Trace outline of stocking onto this background with strips on the diagonal
- Appliqué toe, stars, and snowman (leaving opening for arms) in place referring to photo
- Place batting behind background piece and quilt
- Cut out stocking with ¼" seam allowance
- Cut out stocking lining (stocking pattern reversed) with seam allowance
- Sew right sides together along top edge. Open and press.
- Cut stocking back (pattern reversed) and stocking lining (pattern right side up) and sew right sides together along top edge. Open and press.
- Put two units right sides together and stitch leaving *opening* on bottom of foot **in the lining**
- Clip curves and turn the stocking.
- Put lining into stocking.
- Add a piece of string, ribbon or cloth at back seam for hanging.

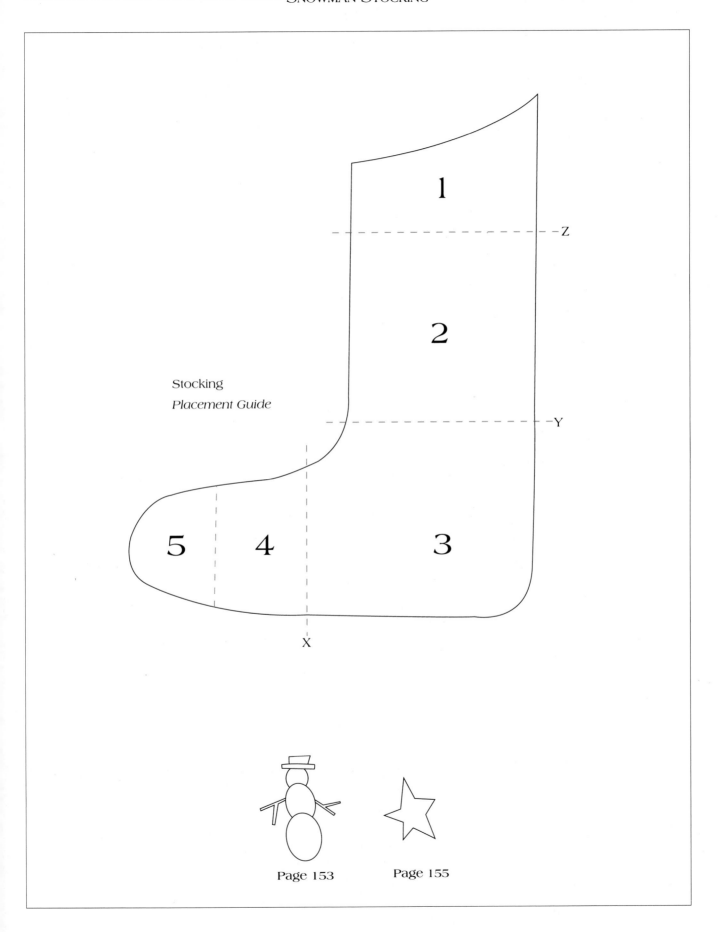

1

Z

2

Stocking
Placement Guide

Y

5 4 3

X

Page 153   Page 155

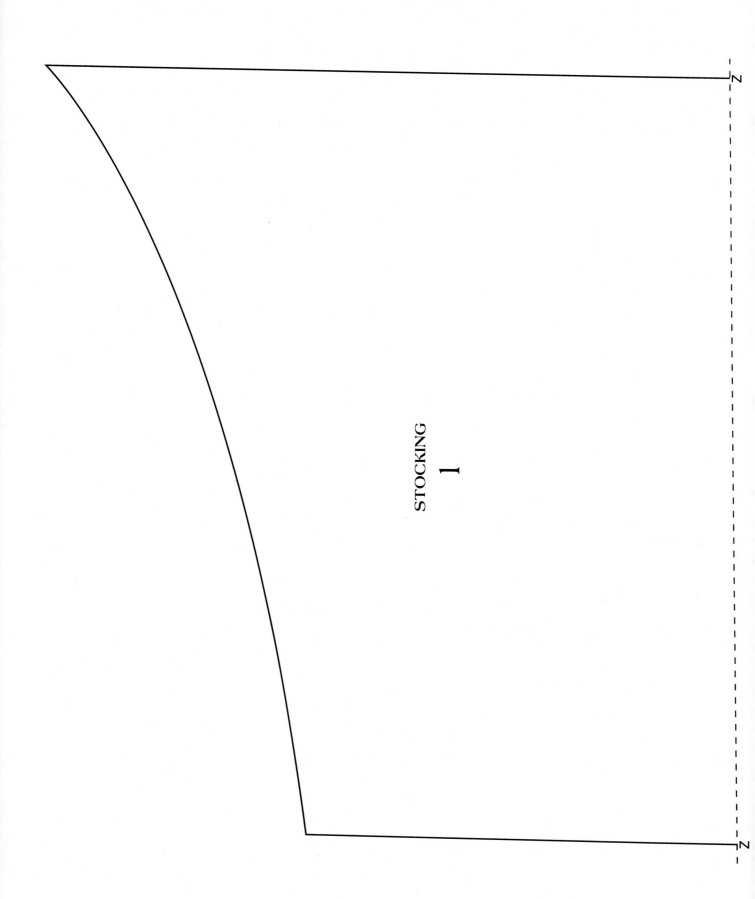

STOCKING
1

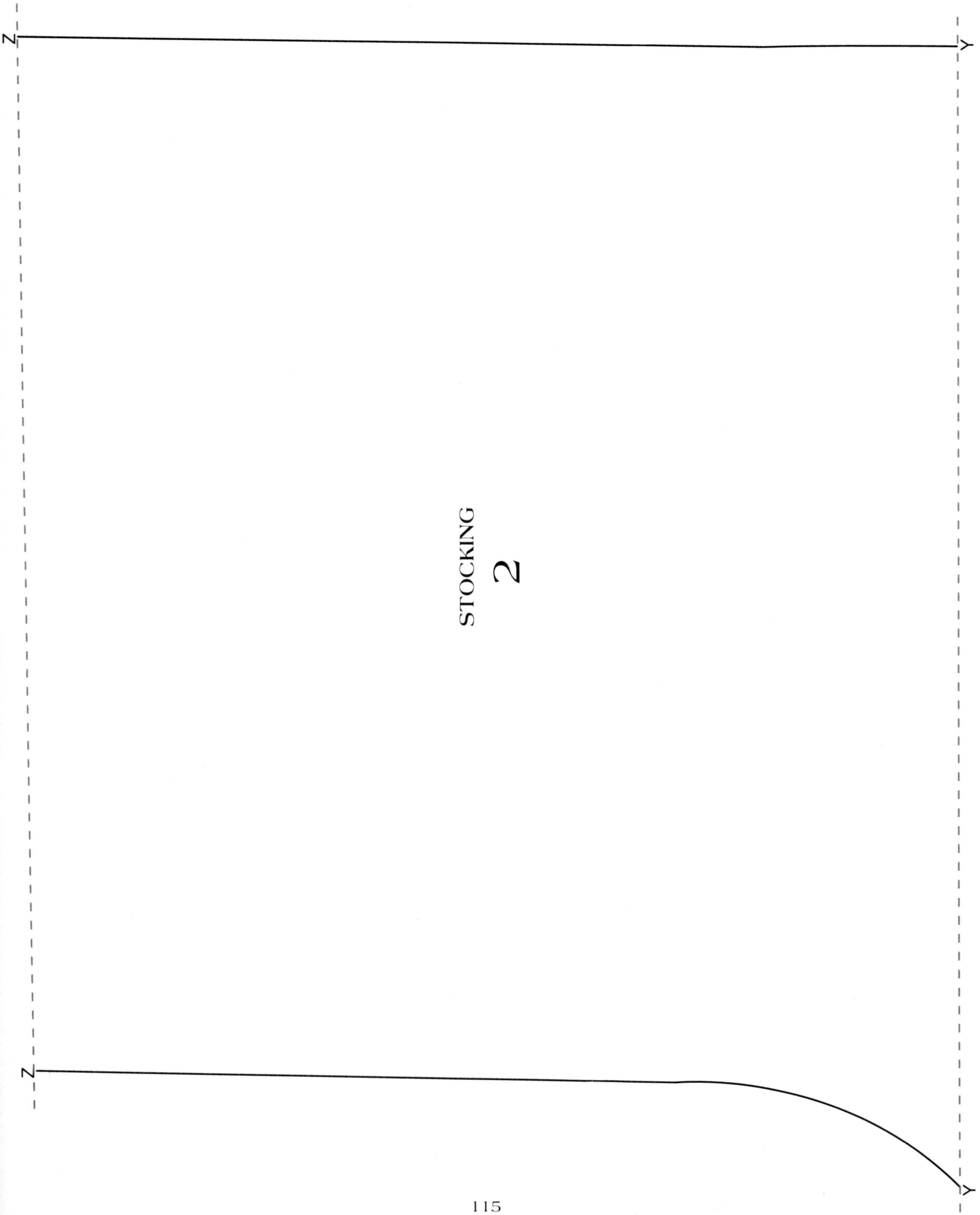

Z

Y

STOCKING
2

Z

Y

STOCKING

3

116

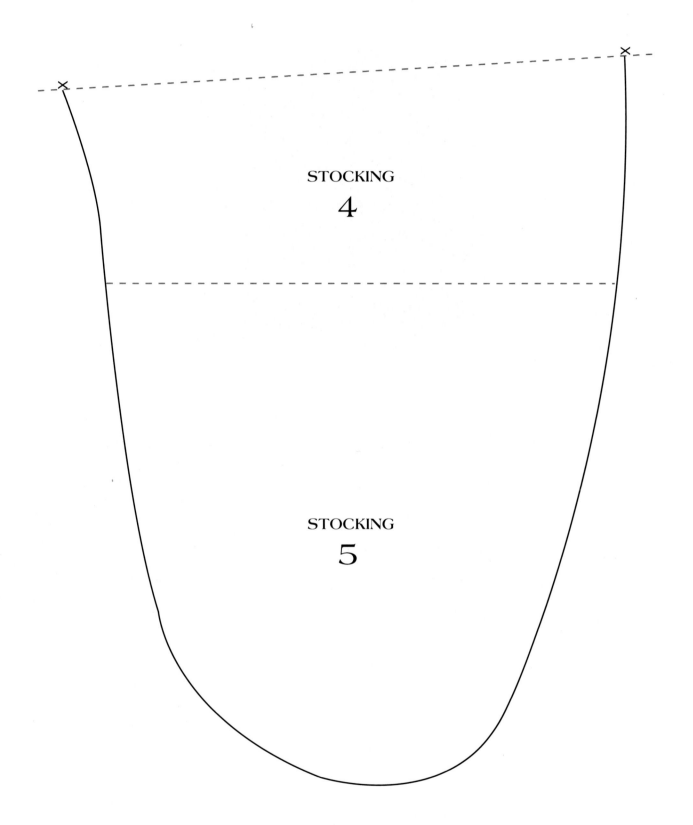

STOCKING

4

STOCKING

5

This quilt was made for two good friends, Peggy and Carlin Sperry who own Pastime Antiques in Jamesport, MO. My house is filled with wonderful furniture from their store that Carlin painstakingly restores. Peggy makes and sells beautiful birdhouses, and the church and the bird in this quilt represent those houses. They are some of the few people outside of my immediate family for whom I have made a quilt because I know they will keep it as well as I would . . . .

SPERRY QUILT
54" x 54" finished size

FABRIC REQUIREMENTS
This is mainly a "scrap" quilt except for the border and the background on some blocks. If you are buying material, ⅛ yd will be sufficient whenever the term "scrap" is used unless otherwise stated.

Border and background
  1¼ yd for border (pieced) and background on blocks
Block #1
  ⅛ yd of 3 darks and 3 lights
  Scraps for centers
Block #2
  Scraps for angel and stars
Block #3 and #5
  Scraps for trees and background
Block #4
  Scraps for Santa and flying geese
  ¼ yd or fat quarter for reindeer
Block #6
  ¼ yd or fat quarter for large portion of flower
  Scraps for flower centers and strip piecing
Block #7
  Scraps for winter solstice and moon blocks
Block #8
  ¼ yd or fat quarter for main body of church
  Scraps for roof, steeple, windows, door, and piecing
Block #9
  Scraps for sunrise and winter solstice blocks
Block #10
  ¼ yd of dark for background
  Scraps for geese
  Scraps for background of geese
Block #11
  Scraps for tree, tree background, and snowman
Block #12
  ¼ yd background material
  Scraps for stars and moon

Block #13
  ¼ yd or fat quarter for bird
  Scraps for bird's wing, perch, and nine-patches
Block #14
  Scraps for winter solstice and background
Block #15
  ¼ yd for house
  ¼ yd for roof
  Scraps for windows, door, chimney, and bottom strip

INSTRUCTIONS (Patterns: pages 124-138, 142-145, 152-157)
• Make 14 – 12" (+sa) blocks and 1 – 12" x 24" blocks to be sewn together as shown in quilt diagram and photo.

BLOCK #1
• Piece four log cabin blocks (center is piece #1 and sew 3 light logs on 2 sides and 3 dark logs on 2 sides). Sew these four blocks together with dark portions in the center, making a 12" block.

BLOCK #2
• Piece 3 stars in following sequence:
      1, 2, 3
      4
      5, 6
      7, 8, 9
• Appliqué wings, horn, and angel to 8" x 12" (+sa) rectangle.
• Combine stars and rectangle as seen in block on page 125 to make 12" (+sa) block.

BLOCK #3
• Piece 3 trees
• Cut 6 dark and 6 light triangles
• Piece in sawtooth pattern
• Combine with trees to make 12" (+sa) block

BLOCK #4
- Cut 8 light triangle #1's and 8 dark triangle #1's and piece together to make 4 large flying geese
- Cut 4 light triangle B's and 2 dark triangle A's and piece together to make small flying geese
- Piece Santa block and appliqué beard in place
- Sew reindeer to 8" x 8" (+sa) square
- Sew large flying geese to square
- Sew small flying geese to Santa block
- Sew two pieces together
- Appliqué Santa's bag in place

BLOCK #5
- Repeat Block #3

BLOCK #6
- Appliqué A's to B's
- Appliqué B's to C's
- Appliqué D, then C to 9" x 9" square
- Cut 9 E's, piece into strip and sew to side of square
- Cut 12 E's, piece into strip and sew to top of square

BLOCK #7
- Cut 4 A's and 4 C's of 7 different background materials
- Cut 1 A, 4 B's and 4 B(r)'s of 7 different materials for winter solstice shape
- Piece to make seven – 4" winter solstice blocks according to block *Placement Guide*
- Appliqué 2 moons to two – 4" (+sa) squares
- Sew together moon squares and winter solstice squares according to block *Placement Guide* to make 12" (+sa) square

BLOCK #8
- Appliqué steeple roof to steeple, church windows, roof, and steeple to church
- Appliqué church to 10" x 10" (+sa) square
- Cut 20 piece B's, 2 light A's, and 2 dark A's
- Piece B's into 2 strips, each strip containing 10 B's – 5 B's long and 2 wide. (See block *Placement Guide*)
- Make 4 patch square of A's
- Sew 1 strip of B's to top of church square (See *Placement Guide*)
- Sew 4 patch of A's to remaining strip of B's (See *Placement Guide*)
- Sew 4 patch and strip to church block and strip (See block *Placement Guide*)

BLOCK #9
- Cut out and piece 2 sunrise blocks (the piece shapes and colors are reverse in one block)
- Sew blocks together side by side to make sunrise
- Cut 4 A's and 4 C's of 2 different background materials for 6" winter solstice blocks
- Cut 1 A, 4 B's and 4B(r)'s of 2 different winter solstice materials
- Piece two 6" winter solstice blocks according to block on page 131
- Sew together winter solstice blocks and sunrise blocks according to block *Placement Guide*.

BLOCK #10
- Cut 4 A's of green background material
- Cut 4 B's, 16 D's, 16 D(r)'s, and 1 E of red background material
- Cut 16 C's for geese (can be different materials)
- Piece block in following suggested sequence (See block *Placement Guide*)
    D, C, D(r). (Sew together 4 sets to make leg of geese)
- Attach B to end of leg (always have geese flying away from B)
    Then, A, leg, A
    Leg, E, leg (geese heading into E)
    A, leg, A
- Sew 3 pieces together according to block *Placement Guide*

BLOCK #11
- Piece tree from block #3
- Cut 2 dark triangles and 2 light triangles from block #3
- Appliqué snowman to 8" x 12" (+sa) rectangle
- Combine tree, snowman, and triangles according to block diagram to make 12" (+sa) square

BLOCK #12
- Cut 44 A's and 44 B's of background material to make eleven – 4" star blocks
- Cut 11 A's and 44 B's of star material
- Piece according to block on page 134.
- Appliqué moon to one – 4" (+sa) square
- Combine eleven – 4" star blocks and 1 moon block to make 12" (+sa) block according to block *Placement Guide*

BLOCK #13

- Appliqué wing to bird
- Appliqué bird and branch to 8" x 12" rectangle
- Piece 3 nine-patches using piece D
- Combine nine-patches and bird according to block *Placement Guide*

BLOCK #14

- Cut 4 A's and 4 C's of background material
- Cut 4 B's, 4 B(r)'s, and 1 A of winter solstice material
- Piece according to block on page 136

BLOCK #15

- Piece house block in following sequence:

    A, B, C

    Sew above to D

    E, F

    G, H, I

    Sew above to D

    J, K, L – sew to house
- Add 1½" x 17" (+sa) strip to bottom of house
- Make 2 courthouse steps blocks
- Starting with center (#1) alternate

    2 light to top and bottom through piece #6

    2 dark to sides through piece #7
- Combine house block with 2 courthouse steps blocks according to block *Placement Guide*

- Assemble Blocks 1-15 according to quilt **Diagram #1** and photo
- Cut 2 – 48" x 3" (+sa) borders
- Cut 2 – 54" x 3" (+sa) borders
- Sew 48" x 3" borders to top and bottom
- Sew 54" x 3" borders to sides
- Quilt and bind.

Block #1

Placement Guide

Each new number is a new template. Sew pieces in numerical order, adding "a" pieces first and then "b" pieces.

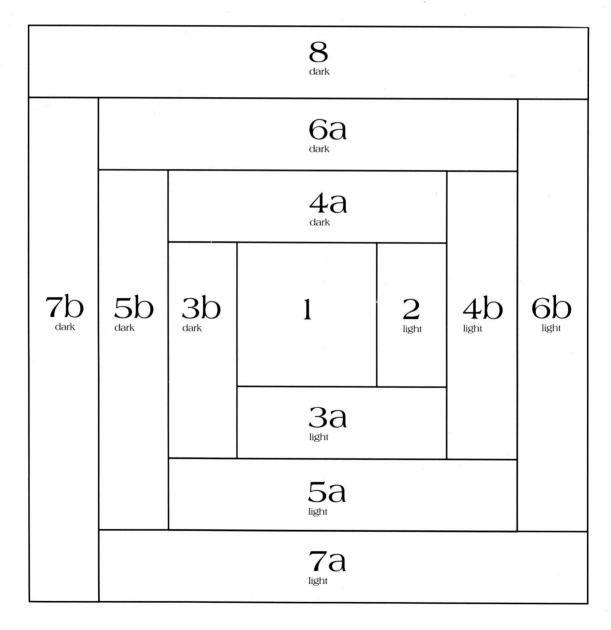

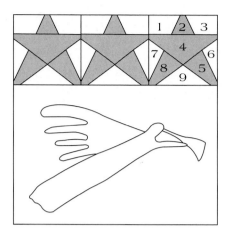

Block #2

Placement Guide

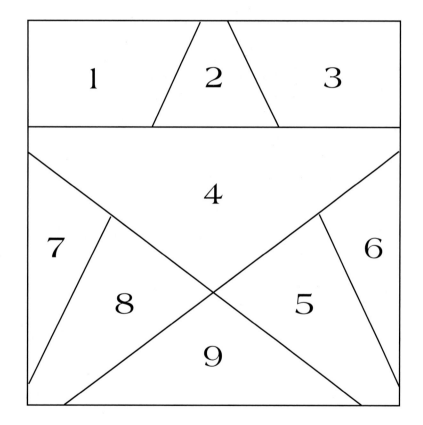

Page 157

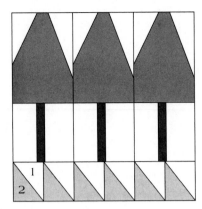

Blocks #3, #5 & #11

Placement Guide

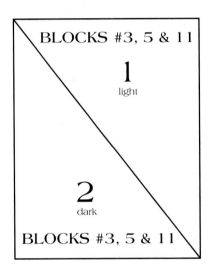

BLOCKS #3, 5 & 11

1
light

2
dark

BLOCKS #3, 5 & 11

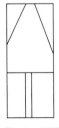

Page 152

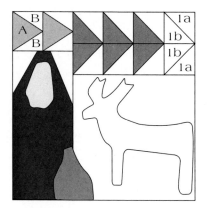

Blocks #4

Placement Guide

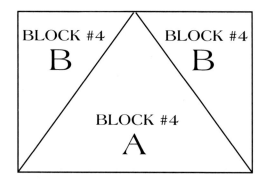

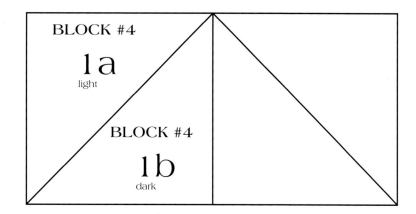

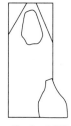

Page 156

Page 154

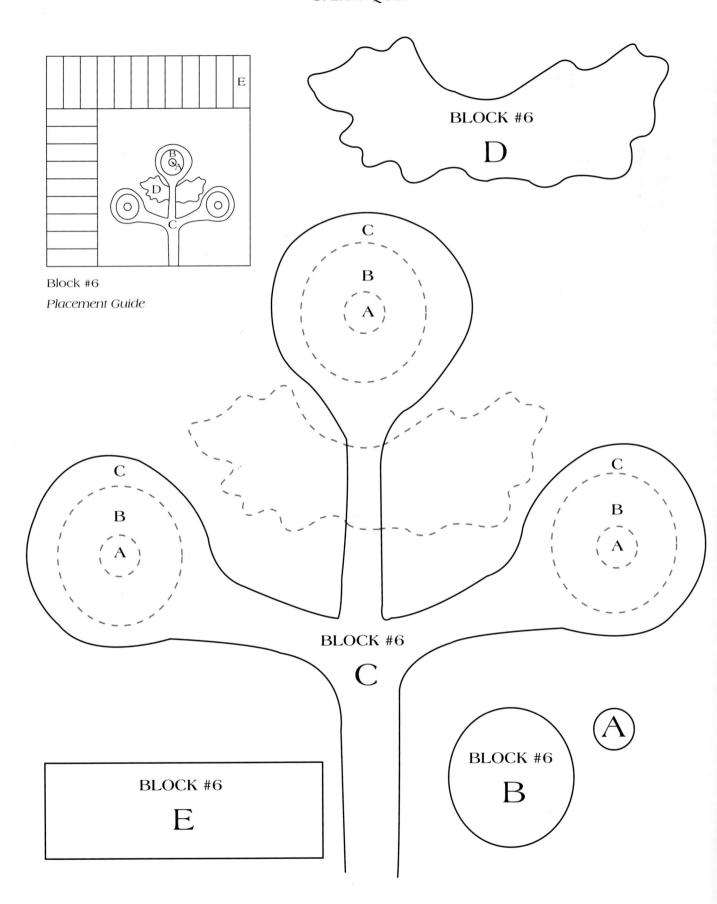

Block #6

Placement Guide

BLOCK #6

D

C

B

A

BLOCK #6

C

C

B

A

C

B

A

BLOCK #6

E

BLOCK #6

B

A

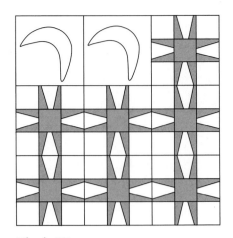

Block #7

Placement Guide

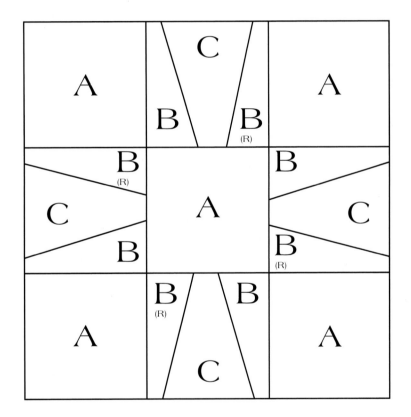

Page 155

129

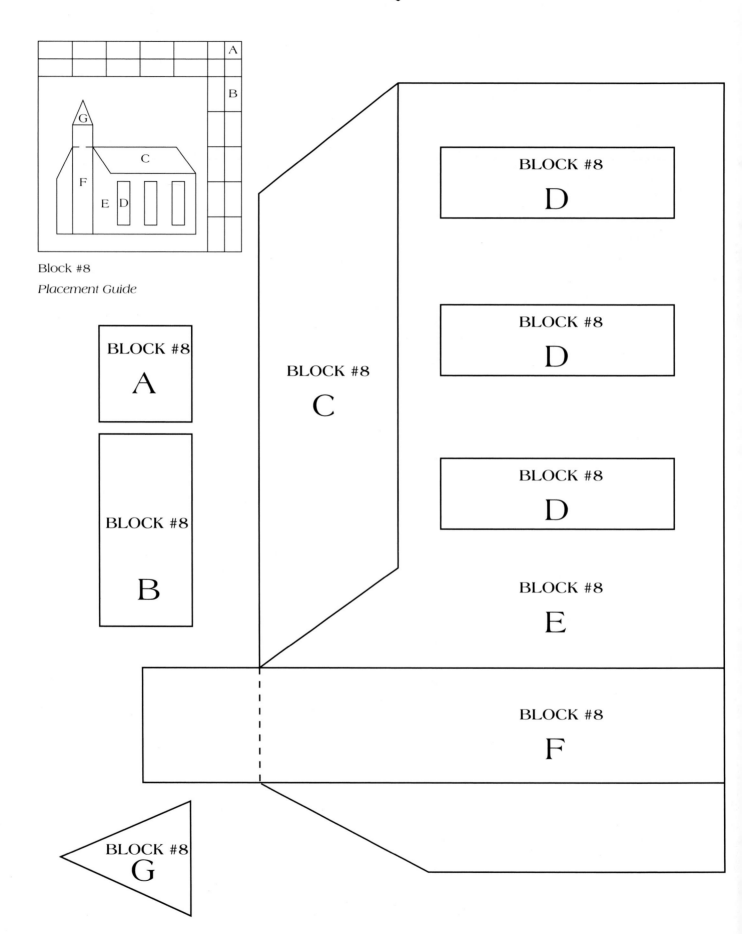

Block #8

Placement Guide

BLOCK #8
A

BLOCK #8
B

BLOCK #8
C

BLOCK #8
D

BLOCK #8
D

BLOCK #8
D

BLOCK #8
E

BLOCK #8
F

BLOCK #8
G

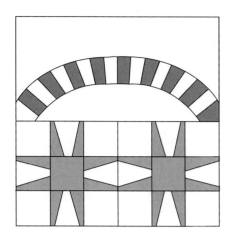

Block #9
Placement Guide

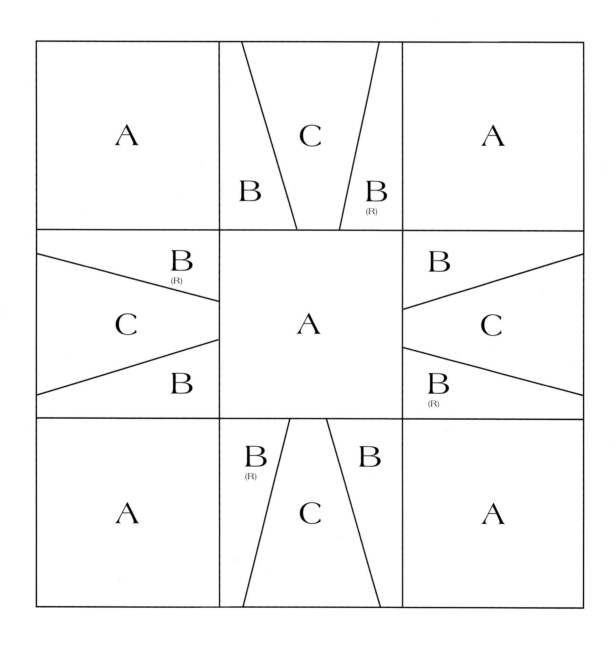

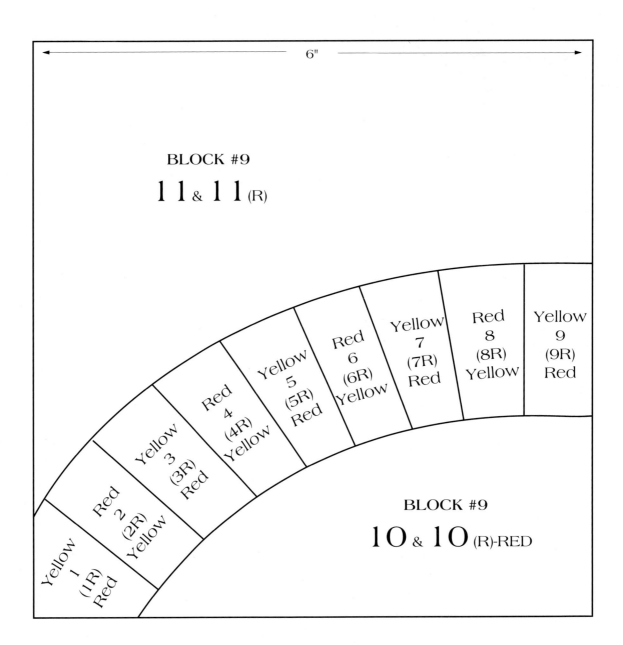

6"

BLOCK #9

11 & 11 (R)

Yellow 1 (1R) Red

Red 2 (2R) Yellow

Yellow 3 (3R) Red

Red 4 (4R) Yellow

Yellow 5 (5R) Red

Red 6 (6R) Yellow

Yellow 7 (7R) Red

Red 8 (8R) Yellow

Yellow 9 (9R) Red

BLOCK #9

10 & 10 (R)-RED

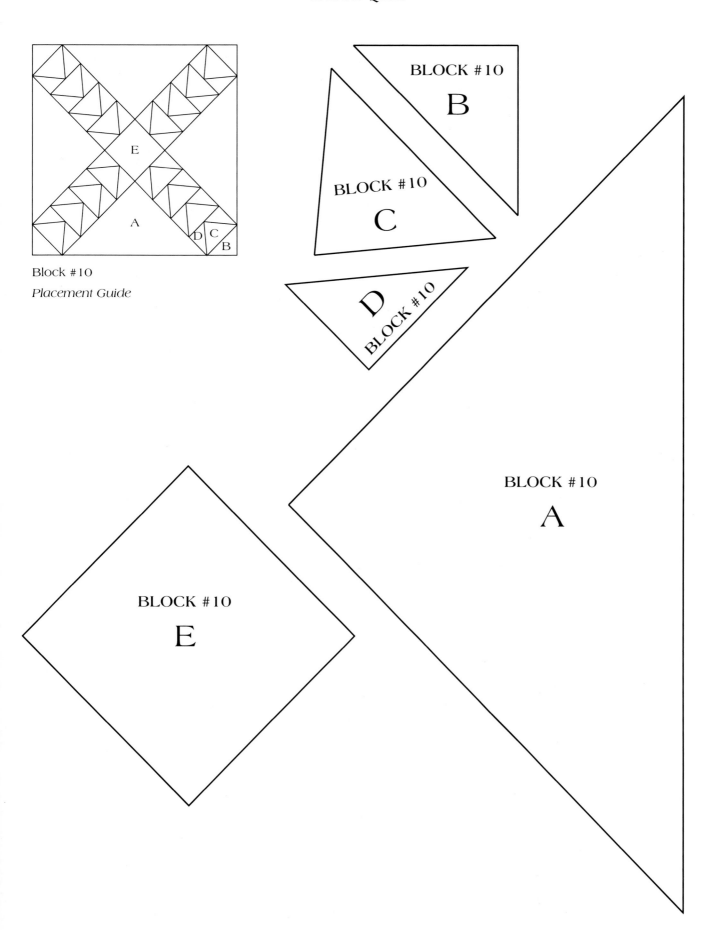

Block #10
Placement Guide

BLOCK #10
B

BLOCK #10
C

BLOCK #10
D

BLOCK #10
A

BLOCK #10
E

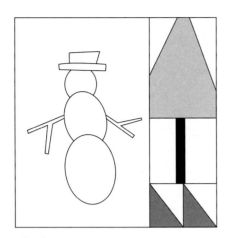

Block #11

Placement Guide

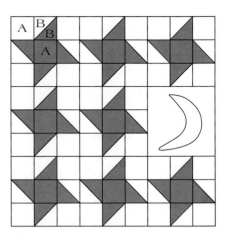

Block #12

Placement Guide

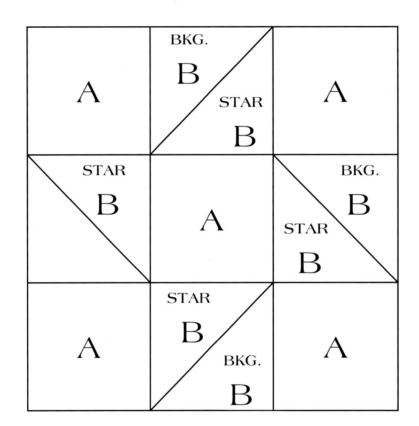

Page 153

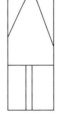

Page 152

Page 126

Page 155

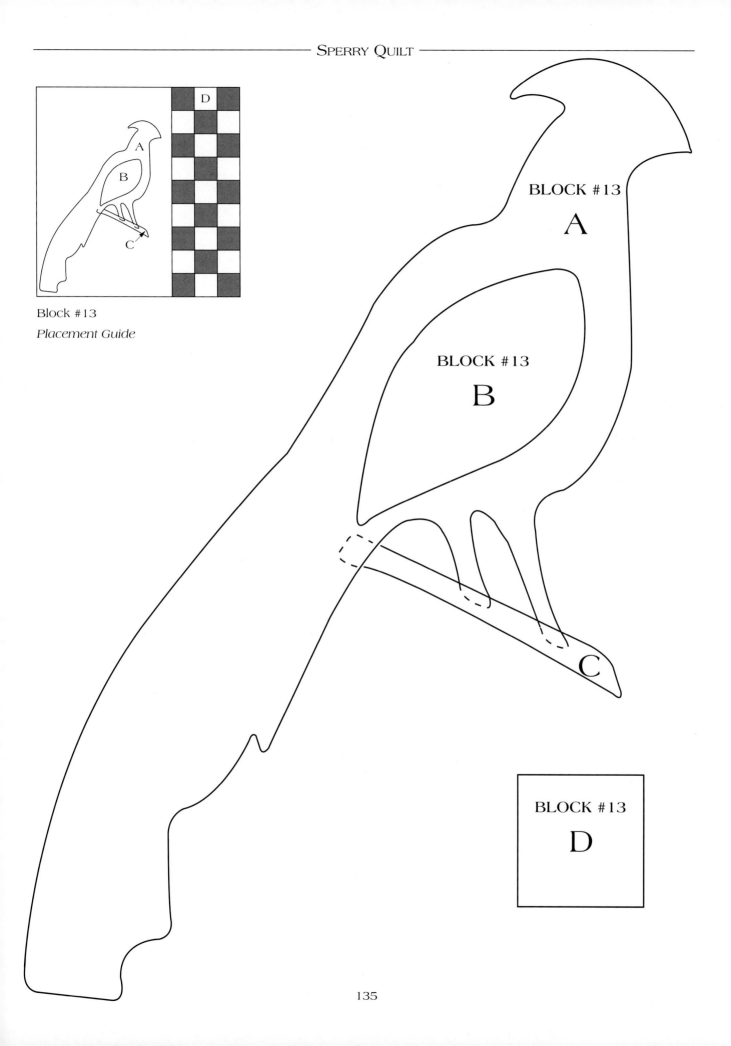

Block #13

Placement Guide

BLOCK #13

A

BLOCK #13

B

BLOCK #13

C

BLOCK #13

D

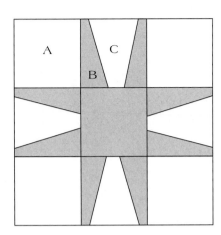

Block #14
Placement Guide

Placement guide only; patterns on page 137

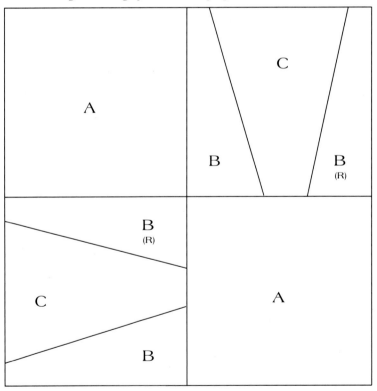

BLOCK #14

A

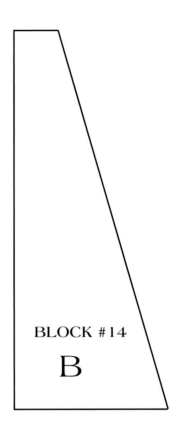

BLOCK #14

B

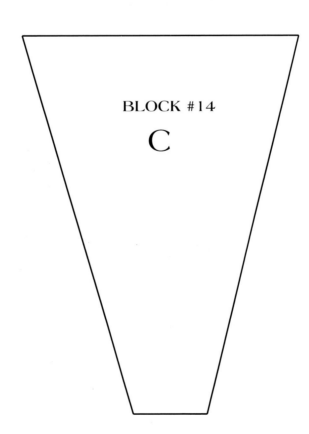

BLOCK #14

C

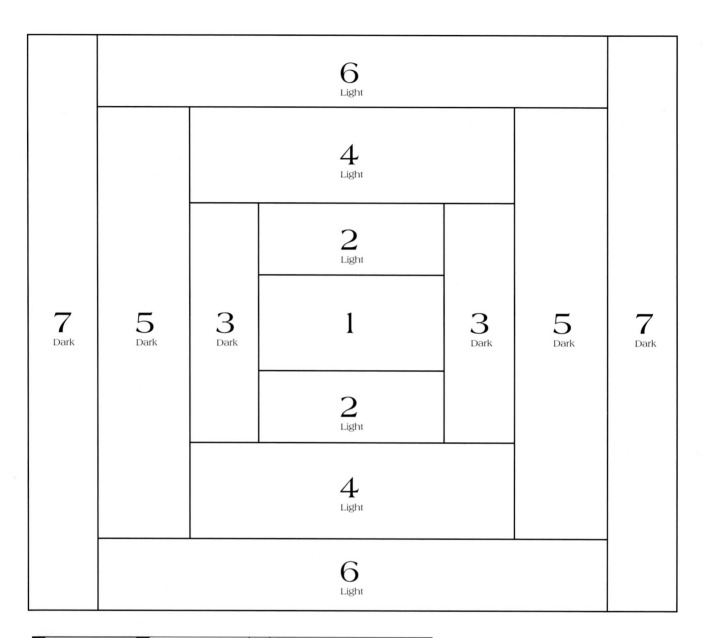

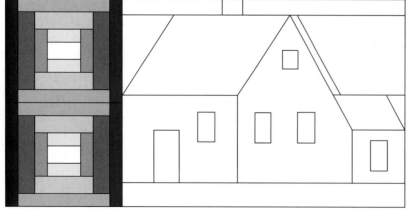

Block #15
Placement Guide

Page 142

Full Quilt Diagram #1

WINTER SOLSTICE (SMALL)
14" x 18" finished size

FABRIC REQUIREMENTS
Scraps for winter solstice blocks
and moon blocks
Scraps for border

INSTRUCTIONS (Patterns: pages 141, 155)
- Cut and piece 9 – 4" (+sa) Winter Solstice blocks
- Cut and piece 1 – 4" (+sa) star block
- Cut 2 – 4" (+sa) background blocks
- Appliqué moons to background blocks
- Sew together blocks in 4 rows of 3 each according to **Diagram**
- Cut 2 – 12" x 1" (+sa) borders
- Cut 2 – 18" x 1" (+sa) borders
- Sew 12" x 1" borders to top and bottom
- Sew 18" x 1" borders to sides
- Quilt and bind.

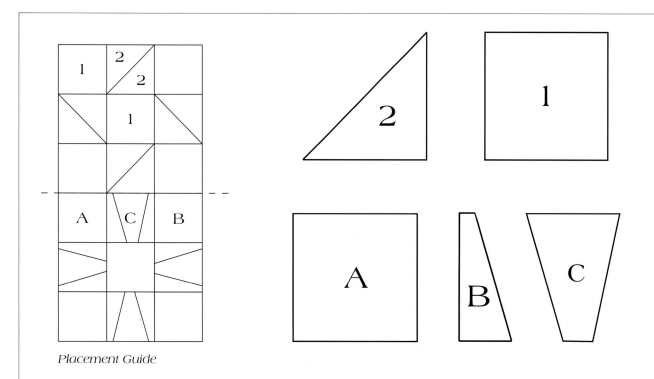

Placement Guide

Full Quilt Diagram

Page 155

141

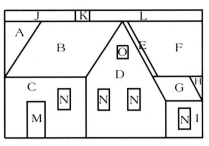

House

Placement Guide

PATTERN:

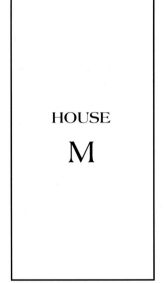

HOUSE

M

HOUSE

K

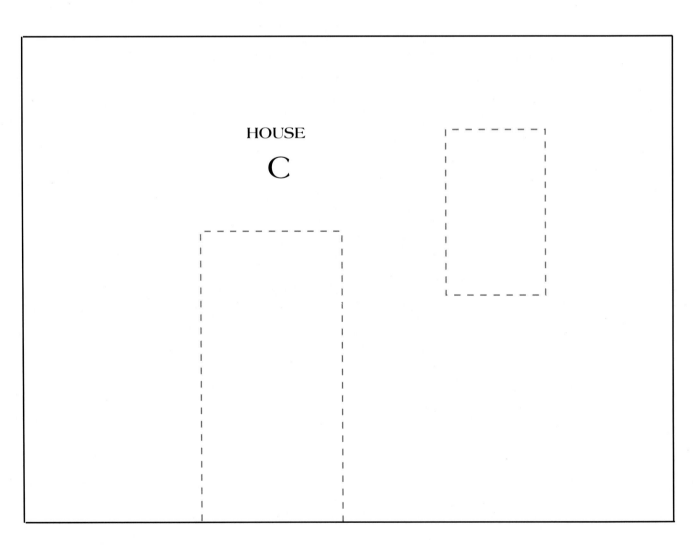

HOUSE

C

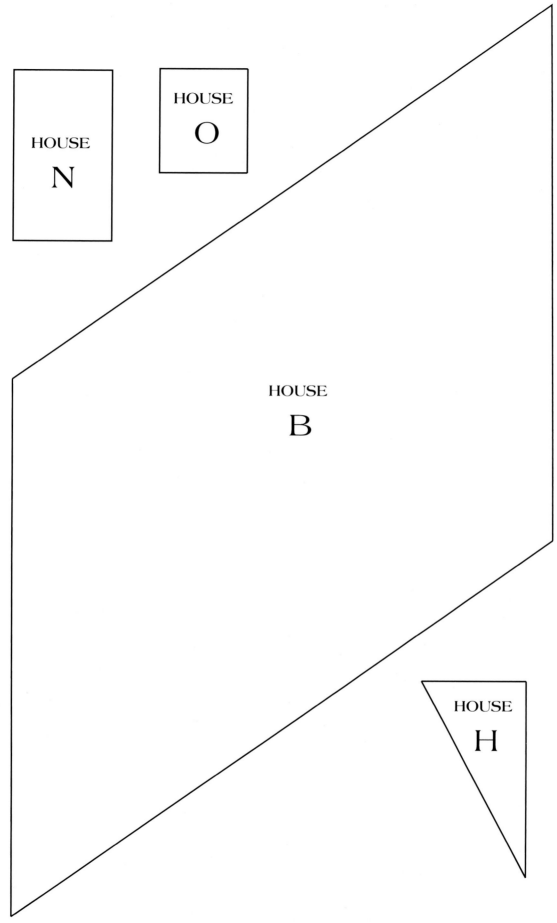

HOUSE
N

HOUSE
O

HOUSE
B

HOUSE
H

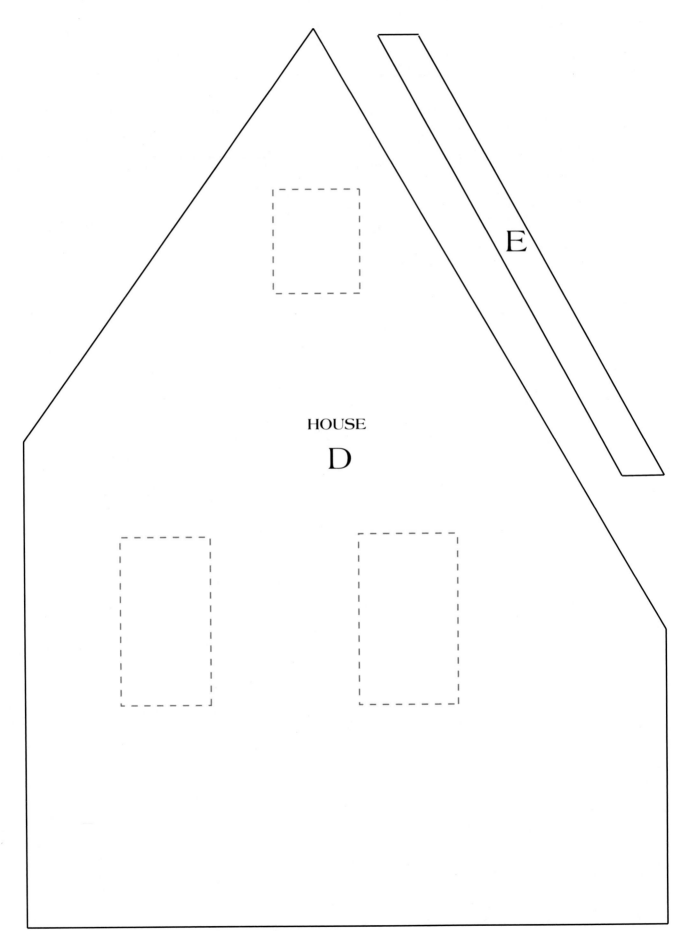

HOUSE

D

E

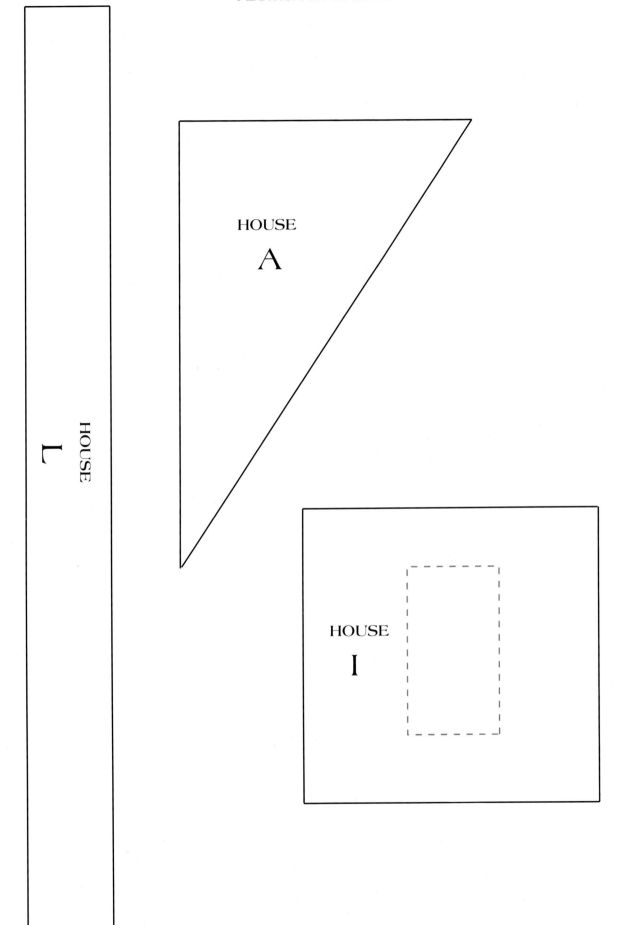

HOUSE

A

HOUSE

L

HOUSE

I

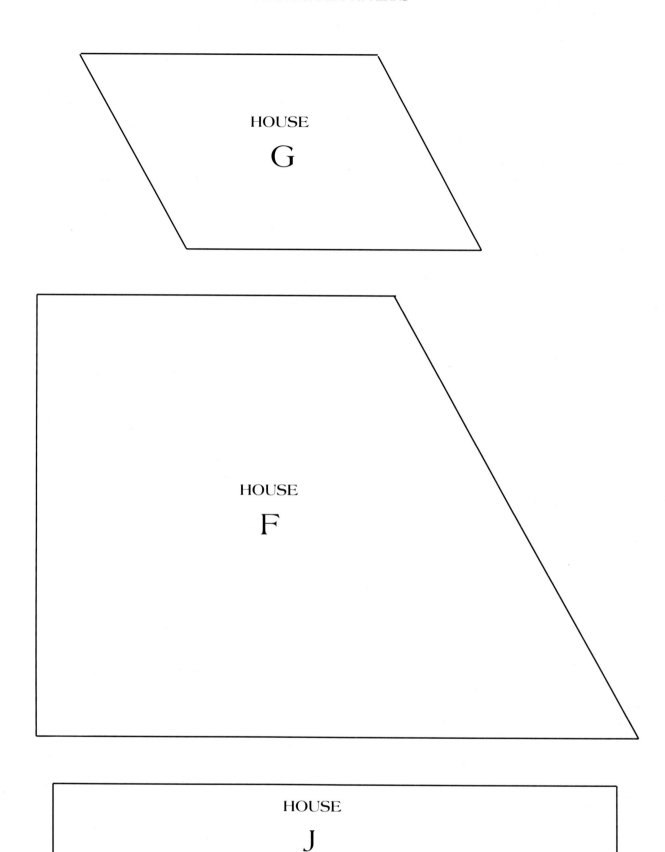

HOUSE

G

HOUSE

F

HOUSE

J

PATTERN:

CADWELL COUNTY – page 42
FALL PLACEMATS – page 62

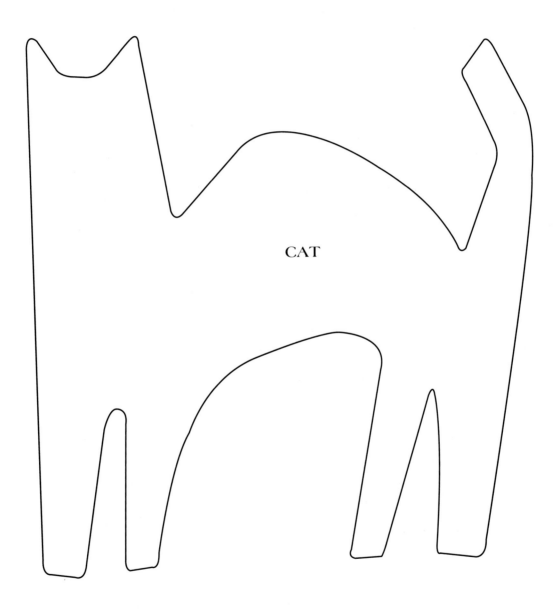

CAT

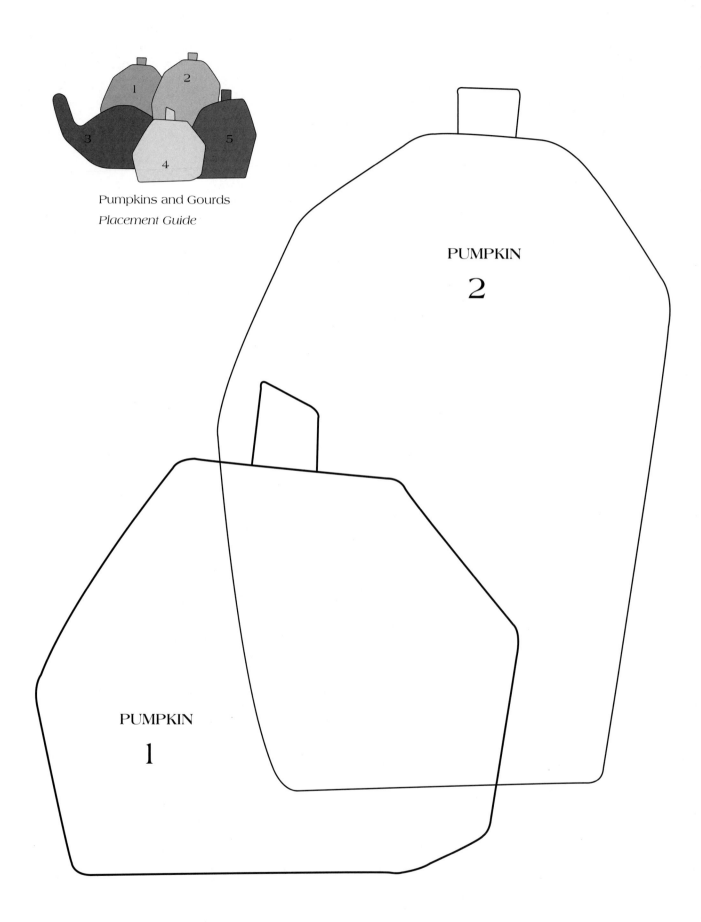

Pumpkins and Gourds
Placement Guide

PUMPKIN

2

PUMPKIN

1

PATTERN:

CADWELL COUNTY – page 42
FALL PLACEMATS – page 62

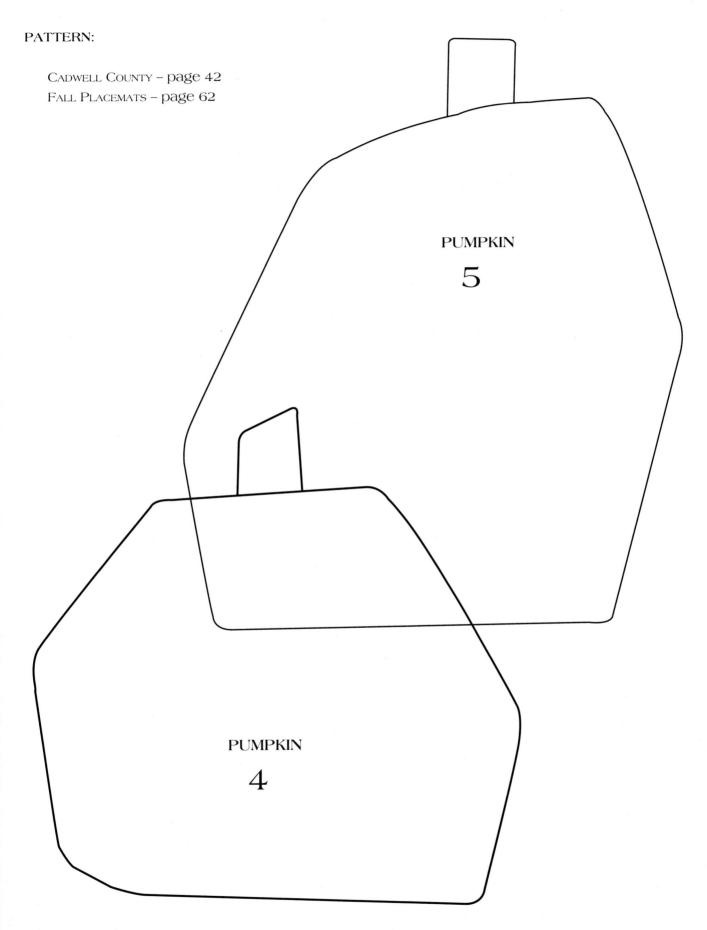

PUMPKIN

5

PUMPKIN

4

PATTERN:

CADWELL COUNTY – page 42
FALL PLACEMATS – page 62

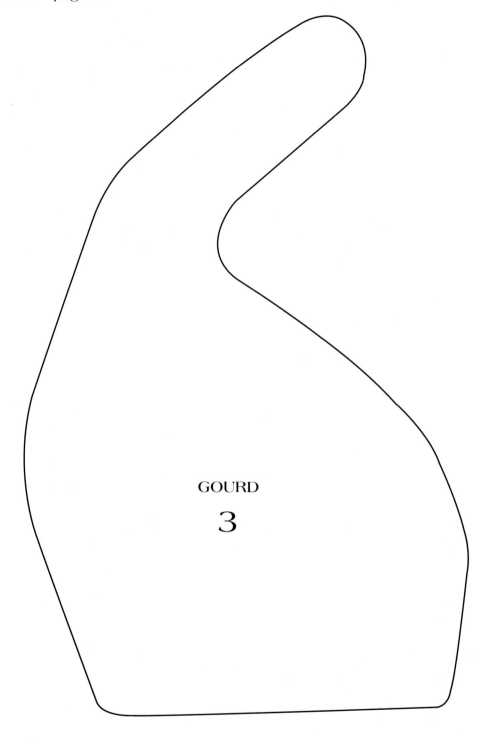

GOURD

3

PATTERN:

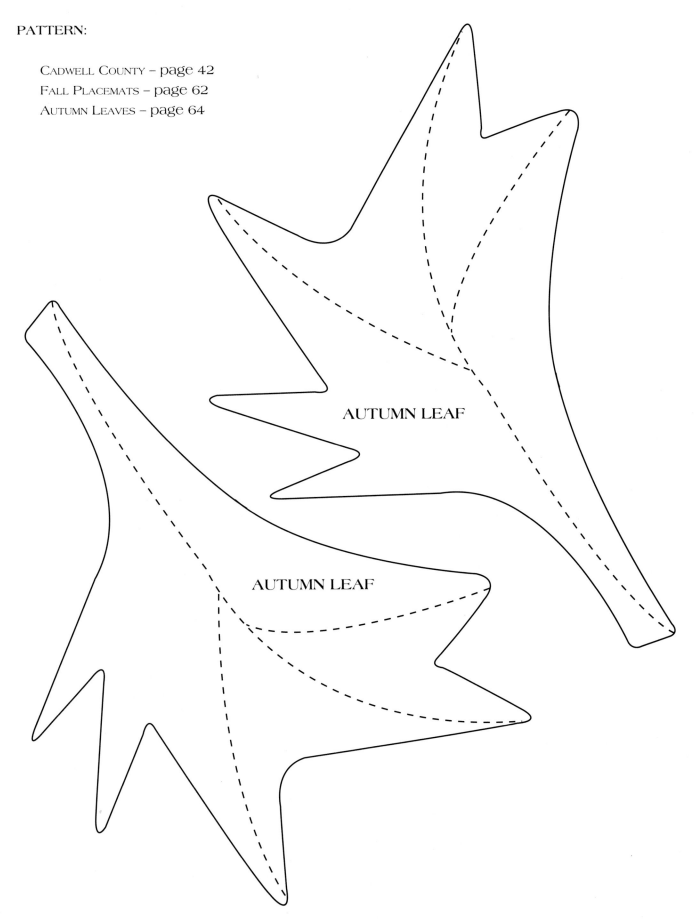

AUTUMN LEAF

AUTUMN LEAF

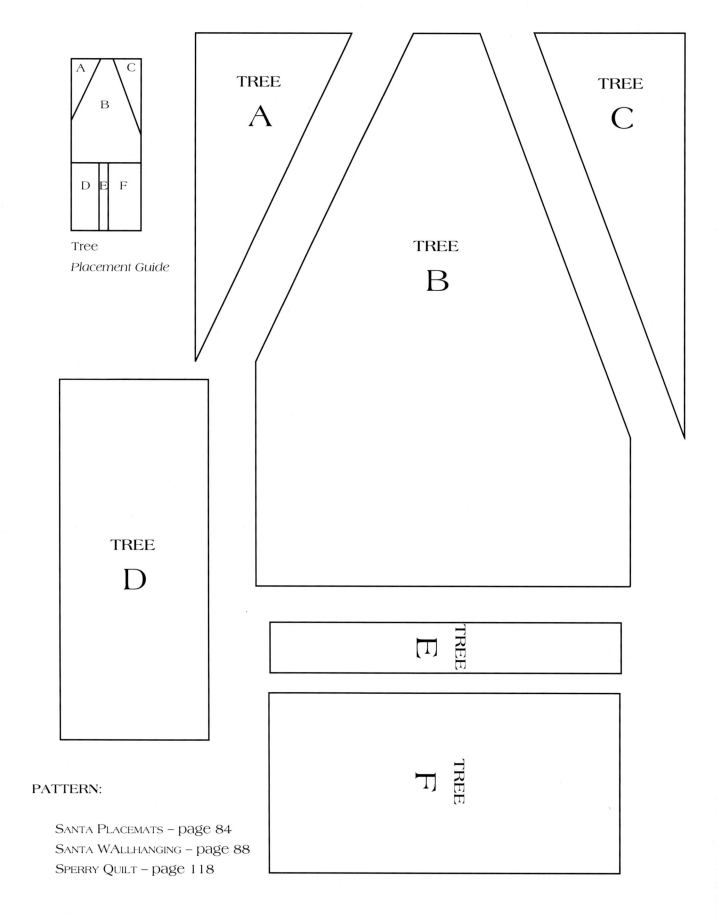

Tree
Placement Guide

TREE
A

TREE
C

TREE
B

TREE
D

TREE
E

TREE
F

PATTERN:

SANTA PLACEMATS – page 84
SANTA WALLHANGING – page 88
SPERRY QUILT – page 118

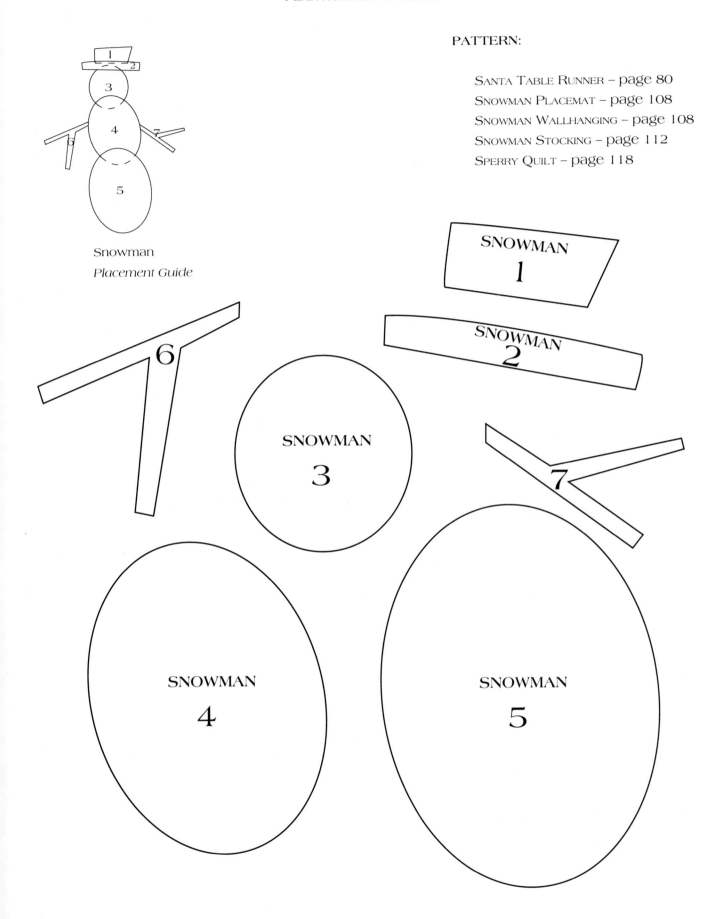

Snowman

Placement Guide

PATTERN:

SNOWMAN 1

SNOWMAN 2

6

7

SNOWMAN 3

SNOWMAN 4

SNOWMAN 5

PATTERN:

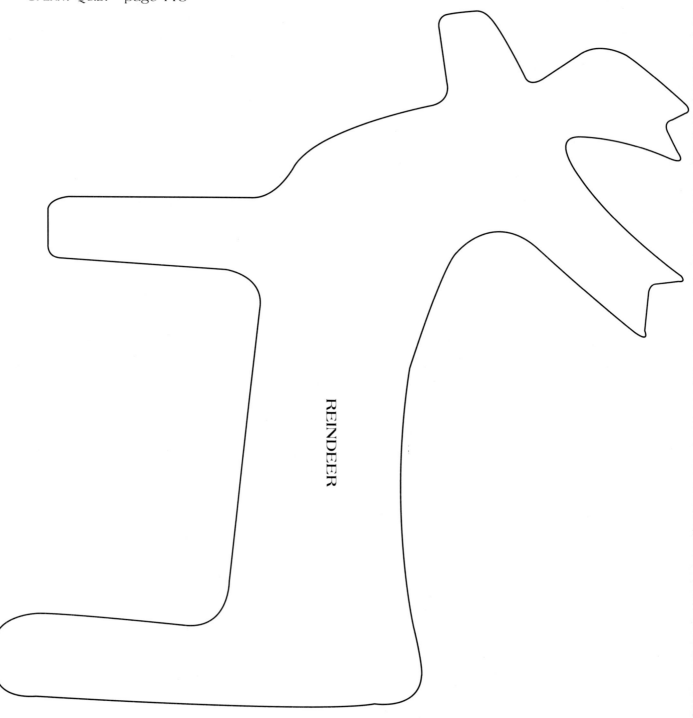

REINDEER

PATTERN:

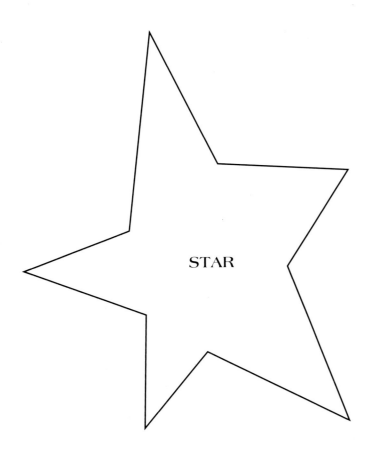

STAR

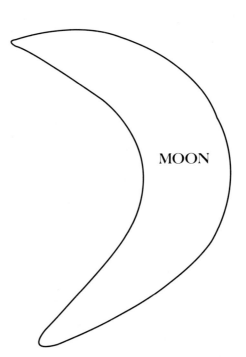

MOON

PATTERN:

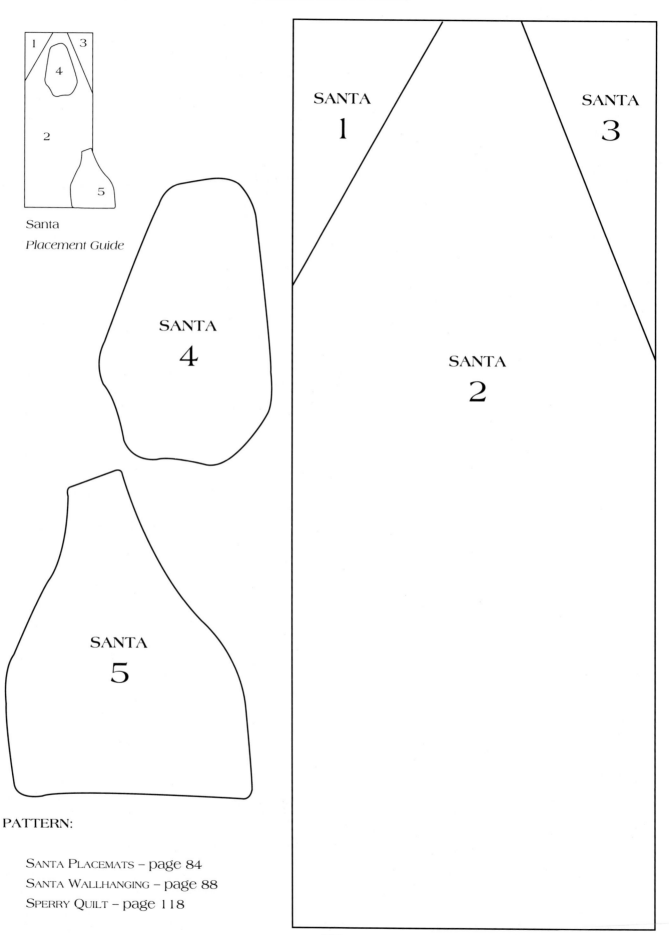

Santa

Placement Guide

SANTA
1

SANTA
3

SANTA
2

SANTA
4

SANTA
5

PATTERN:

SANTA PLACEMATS – page 84

SANTA WALLHANGING – page 88

SPERRY QUILT – page 118

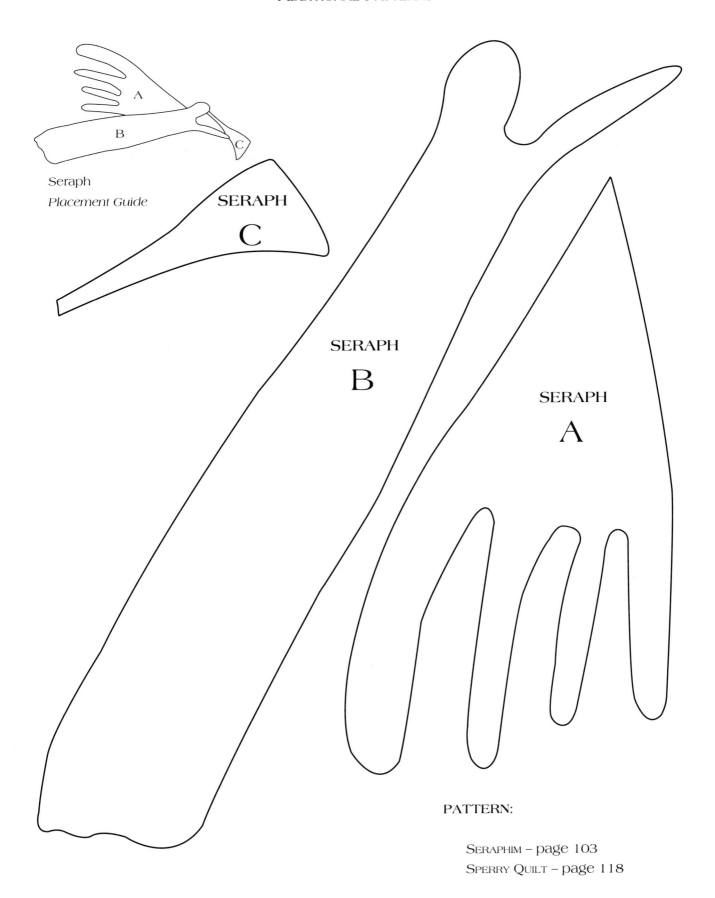

Seraph

Placement Guide

SERAPH

C

SERAPH

B

SERAPH

A

PATTERN:

SERAPHIM – page 103
SPERRY QUILT – page 118

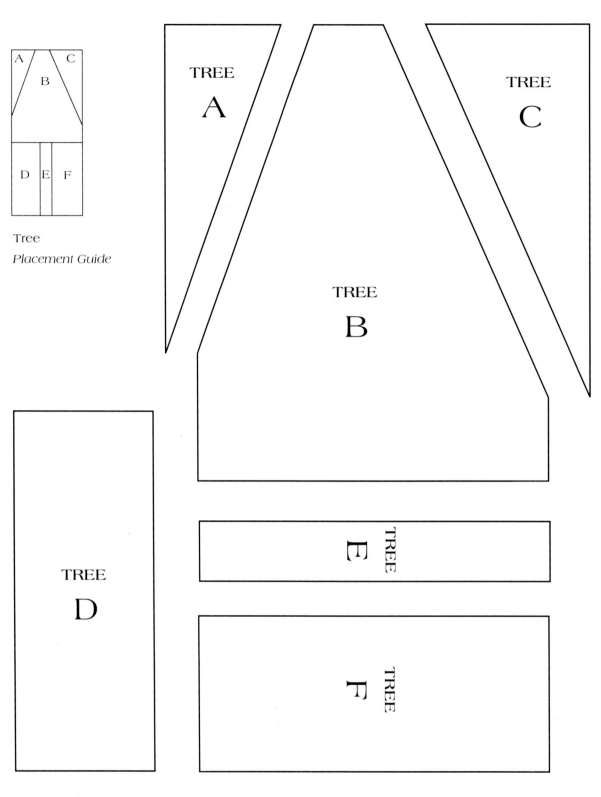

Tree
Placement Guide

TREE
A

TREE
C

TREE
B

TREE
D

TREE
E

TREE
F

PATTERN:

SANTA TABLE RUNNER – page 80

158

References

Women of the 14th Moon
Writings on Menopause
Essays by Joan Borton & Maureen Williams
Edited by Dena Taylor and Amber Coverdale Sumrall
The Crossing Press
Freedom, CA 95019
Copyright 1991

Plant Dreaming Deep
May Sarton
W. W. Norton & Co.
New York . London
Copyright 1968

Journal of a Solitude
May Sarton
W. W. Norton & Co.
New York . London
Copyright 1973

Women Who Run With the Wolves
Clarissa Pinkola Estés, Ph.D.
Ballentine Books
New York
Copyright 1992

~American Quilter's Society~
dedicated to publishing books for today's quilters

The following AQS publications are currently available:

- **Adapting Architectural Details for Quilts,** Carol Wagner, #2282: AQS, 1991, 88 pages, softbound, $12.95
- **American Beauties: Rose & Tulip Quilts,** Gwen Marston & Joe Cunningham, #1907: AQS, 1988, 96 pages, softbound, $14.95
- **America's Pictorial Quilts,** Caron L. Mosey, #1662: AQS, 1985, 112 pages, hardbound, $19.95
- **Applique Designs: My Mother Taught Me to Sew,** Faye Anderson, #2121: AQS, 1990, 80 pages, softbound, $12.95
- **Arkansas Quilts: Arkansas Warmth,** Arkansas Quilter's Guild, Inc., #1908: AQS, 1987, 144 pages, hardbound, $24.95
- **The Art of Hand Applique,** Laura Lee Fritz, #2122: AQS, 1990, 80 pages, softbound, $14.95
- **...Ask Helen More About Quilting Designs,** Helen Squire, #2099: AQS, 1990, 54 pages, 17 x 11, spiral-bound, $14.95
- **Award-Winning Quilts & Their Makers: Vol. I, The Best of AQS Shows – 1985-1987,** #2207: AQS, 1991, 232 pages, softbound, $24.95
- **Award-Winning Quilts & Their Makers: Vol. II, The Best of AQS Shows – 1988-1989,** #2354: AQS, 1992, 176 pages, softbound, $24.95
- **Award-Winning Quilts & Their Makers: Vol. III, The Best of AQS Shows – 1990-1991,** #3425: AQS, 1993, 180 pages, softbound, $24.95
- **Classic Basket Quilts,** Elizabeth Porter & Marianne Fons, #2208: AQS, 1991, 128 pages, softbound, $16.95
- **A Collection of Favorite Quilts,** Judy Florence, #2119: AQS, 1990, 136 pages, softbound, $18.95
- **Creative Machine Art,** Sharee Dawn Roberts, #2355: AQS, 1992, 142 pages, 9 x 9, softbound, $24.95
- **Dear Helen, Can You Tell Me?...all about quilting designs,** Helen Squire, #1820: AQS, 1987, 51 pages, 17 x 11, spiral-bound, $12.95
- **Dye Painting!,** Ann Johnston, #3399: AQS, 1992, 88 pages, softbound, $19.95
- **Dyeing & Overdyeing of Cotton Fabrics,** Judy Mercer Tescher, #2030: AQS, 1990, 54 pages, softbound, $9.95
- **Encyclopedia of Pieced Quilt Patterns,** compiled by Barbara Brackman, #3468: AQS, 1993, 552 pages, hardbound, $34.95
- **Flavor Quilts for Kids to Make: Complete Instructions for Teaching Children to Dye, Decorate & Sew Quilts,** Jennifer Amor #2356: AQS, 1991, 120 pages, softbound, $12.95
- **From Basics to Binding: A Complete Guide to Making Quilts,** Karen Kay Buckley, #2381: AQS, 1992, 160 pages, softbound, $16.95
- **Fun & Fancy Machine Quiltmaking,** Lois Smith, #1982: AQS, 1989, 144 pages, softbound, $19.95
- **Gallery of American Quilts 1830-1991: Book III,** #3421: AQS, 1992, 128 pages, softbound, $19.95
- **The Grand Finale: A Quilter's Guide to Finishing Projects,** Linda Denner, #1924: AQS, 1988, 96 pages, softbound, $14.95
- **Heirloom Miniatures,** Tina M. Gravatt, #2097: AQS, 1990, 64 pages, softbound, $9.95
- **Infinite Stars,** Gayle Bong, #2283: AQS, 1992, 72 pages, softbound, $12.95
- **The Ins and Outs: Perfecting the Quilting Stitch,** Patricia J. Morris, #2120: AQS, 1990, 96 pages, softbound, $9.95
- **Irish Chain Quilts: A Workbook of Irish Chains & Related Patterns,** Joyce B. Peaden, #1906: AQS, 1988, 96 pages, softbound, $14.95
- **The Log Cabin Returns to Kentucky: Quilts from the Pilgrim/Roy Collection,** Gerald Roy and Paul Pilgrim, #3329: AQS, 1992, 36 pages, 9 x 7, softbound, $12.95
- **Marbling Fabrics for Quilts: A Guide for Learning & Teaching,** Kathy Fawcett & Carol Shoaf, #2206: AQS, 1991, 72 pages, softbound, $12.95
- **More Projects and Patterns: A Second Collection of Favorite Quilts,** Judy Florence, #3330: AQS, 1992, 152 pages, softbound, $18.95
- **Nancy Crow: Quilts and Influences,** Nancy Crow, #1981: AQS, 1990, 256 pages, 9 x 12, hardcover, $29.95
- **Nancy Crow: Work in Transition,** Nancy Crow, #3331: AQS, 1992, 32 pages, 9 x 10, softbound, $12.95
- **New Jersey Quilts – 1777 to 1950: Contributions to an American Tradition,** The Heritage Quilt Project of New Jersey; text by Rachel Cochran, Rita Erickson, Natalie Hart & Barbara Schaffer, #3332: AQS, 1992, 256 pages, softbound, $29.95
- **No Dragons on My Quilt,** Jean Ray Laury with Ritva Laury & Lizabeth Laury, #2153: AQS, 1990, 52 pages, hardcover, $12.95
- **Oklahoma Heritage Quilts,** Oklahoma Quilt Heritage Project #2032: AQS, 1990, 144 pages, softbound, $19.95
- **Old Favorites in Miniature,** Tina Gravatt #3469: AQS, 1993, 104 pages, softbound, $15.95
- **Quilt Groups Today: Who They Are, Where They Meet, What They Do, and How to Contact Them; A Complete Guide for 1992-1993,** #3308: AQS, 1992, 336 pages, softbound, $14.95
- **Quilt Registry,** Lynne Fritz, #2380: AQS, 1992, 80 pages, hardbound, $9.95
- **Quilting Patterns from Native American Designs,** Dr. Joyce Mori, #3467: AQS, 1993, 80 pages, softbound, $12.95
- **Quilting with Style: Principles for Great Pattern Design,** Gwen Marston & Joe Cunningham #3470: AQS, 1993, 192 pages, 9 x 12, hardbound, $24.95
- **Quiltmaker's Guide: Basics & Beyond,** Carol Doak, #2284: AQS, 1992, 208 pages, softbound, $19.95
- **Quilts: Old & New, A Similar View,** Paul D. Pilgrim and Gerald E. Roy, #3715: AQS, 1993, 40 pages, softbound, $12.95
- **Quilts: The Permanent Collection – MAQS,** #2257: AQS, 1991, 100 pages, 10 x 6½, softbound, $9.95
- **Seasons of the Heart & Home: Quilts for Summer Days,** Jan Patek, #3761: AQS, 1993, 160 pages, softbound, $18.95
- **Sensational Scrap Quilts,** Darra Duffy Williamson, #2357: AQS, 1992, 152 pages, softbound, $24.95
- **Sets & Borders,** Gwen Marston & Joe Cunningham, #1821: AQS, 1987, 104 pages, softbound, $14.95
- **Show Me Helen...How to Use Quilting Designs,** Helen Squire, #3375: AQS, 1993, 155 pages, softbound, $15.95
- **Somewhere in Between: Quilts and Quilters of Illinois,** Rita Barrow Barber, #1790: AQS, 1986, 78 pages, softbound, $14.95
- **Stenciled Quilts for Christmas,** Marie Monteith Sturmer, #2098: AQS, 1990, 104 pages, softbound, $14.95
- **A Treasury of Quilting Designs,** Linda Goodmon Emery, #2029: AQS, 1990, 80 pages, 14 x 11, spiral-bound, $14.95
- **Wonderful Wearables: A Celebration of Creative Clothing,** Virginia Avery, #2286: AQS, 1991, 184 pages, softbound, $24.95

These books can be found in local bookstores and quilt shops. If you are unable to locate a title in your area, you can order by mail from AQS, P.O. Box 3290, Paducah, KY 42002-3290. Please add $1 for the first book and 40¢ for each additional one to cover postage and handling. (International orders please add $1.50 for the first book and $1 for each additional one.)